# Heal your chakras
# ...heal your life

Life is full of wonder but you have to open your eyes to see it. I did this in my childhood and discovered the natural ways to bring health and harmony to the body. After discovering the healing benefits of plants I moved on to discover and train in other forms of healing.

Now I practice these healing techniques at my wellness clinic in Spain. This book is an offering to open your eyes to the wonder that is out there at your fingertips to bring more inner peace into your life.

For once we have inner peace everything else falls into place.

At times you may think you will never make it and are being punished for some forgotten sin you must have committed. You are not being punished, you are being guided to become the best that you can be. We are never given more than we can handle. The old saying, 'What doesn't kill us makes us stronger!' is so true. We always find a way. We draw on that hidden inner strength. So embrace life and its myriad of challenges and know that we truly are blessed to be here.

Use this book with my blessings and I hope it helps you on your pathway.

**All Rights Reserved**

Except for short extracts for credited quotation or review, the contents of this book may not be reproduced in any form, without the written permission of the author. All sources for copyrighted images and material have given permission and have been acknowledged, with thanks.

©2016 Cover Copyright Gaile Griffin Peers and Tamsin German

©2016 Tamsin German

Tamsin German asserts her moral rights

First published in Great Britain in 2016
by Light My Way Publishing UK

A CIP Catalogue record of this book is available from the British Library

Paperback Edition ISBN 978-0-9954758-0-9
eBook ISBN 978-0-9954758-1-6

eBook Edition ISBN 978
FIRST PAPERBACK EDITION

Published by Light My Way Publishing, Avon Dassett, Southam

Printed in England by The Lightning Source Group

www.TamsinGerman.com

# Heal your chakras
# ...heal your life

An easy to follow self help guide to health and happiness.

# By
# Tamsin German

I dedicate this book to my lovely children Ross and Esperanza and my mum and brother who gave me the strength to get through my bad times.

**You are all forever in my heart**

# Preface

This book is devoted to bringing love and light into your life.

It is a journey of discovery. A 'discovery' about yourself. Once we know who we truly are, only then can we begin to embrace life to its fullest. Often we just cruise through life thinking that all is well in ours. For some, this may be true but for the majority of us, it isn't.

Life has many challenges and we have a tendency as humans to close off those areas we don't want to deal with. This, unfortunately, only puts the problem on hold; at some point it will resurface and you will have to face it again. Many choose continually to ignore the challenges and, over time, they are left wondering why their health fails. They are 'good people'; they 'help others', so why are they being punished by ill health? The answer is simple my friend; the problems are self-created.

Challenges come into our life for a reason. They help us to grow and evolve as a spiritual being. When we push them aside they create an imbalance in the body. At first the imbalances will be small and create little effect. But over time the imbalance will become greater, eventually leading to more serious health issues. We are energy and, as such, we need to ebb and flow like the tide. Remember we are souls, inhabiting a human body.

So I offer this book as a tool to help you realise your own healing pathway.

**Tamsin xx**

# Contents

Preface ..................................................................................... 7
Contents .................................................................................. 9
My Journey ............................................................................ 15
Part 1 Understanding what we are......................................... 21
    The building blocks of life ............................................. 23
    The aura and chakra systems......................................... 27
    The seven main chakras and their locations................. 29
        The first layer or Etheric Body.......................... 30
        The second layer or the Emotional Body ......... 31
        The third layer or the Mental Body.................. 33
        The fourth layer or Astral Level........................ 34
        The fifth or Etheric Template Body .................. 35
        The sixth or the Celestial Body......................... 36
        The seventh or Causal Body .............................. 37
    The seven main chakras.................................................. 39
        Base Chakra ....................................................... 40
        Sacral Chakra .................................................... 41
        Solar Plexus Chakra .......................................... 43
        Heart Chakra ..................................................... 44
        Throat Chakra.................................................... 45

Third Eye Chakra ................................................46

Crown Chakra ....................................................47

The Major Chakras and their associations in the body. ...................................................................48

The Lower Chakras .............................................49

Chart showing the minor chakras and their associations in the body ..........................52

Additional chakras .............................................53

Endocrine glands ......................................................56

The Adrenal Glands ...........................................56

Our thoughts ...and their real importance! ...................65

# Part 2 Self-help section ............................................ 69

Crystals ......................................................................71

How to use crystals ...................................................73

Choosing Crystals .....................................................75

Crystals and the Zodiac ....................................75

Caring for your crystals. ...........................................78

Programming your crystal .......................................80

Crystal list .................................................................81

Agate ..................................................................81

Amazonite .........................................................84

Amber ................................................................85

Amethyst ...........................................................86

Apatite ...............................................................87

Aquamarine ......................................................89

Aragonite ..........................................................90

Aventurine .................................................................. 91

Azurite ...................................................................... 93

Black Tourmaline ...................................................... 94

Bloodstone .............................................................. 95

Calcite ...................................................................... 96

Carnelian ................................................................. 99

Celestite ................................................................ 100

Chalcedony ........................................................... 101

Charoite ................................................................ 103

Chrysoprase .......................................................... 104

Citrine ................................................................... 105

Diamond ............................................................... 106

Emerald ................................................................ 107

Fluorite ................................................................. 108

Garnet (red) .......................................................... 110

Hematite .............................................................. 111

Howlite ................................................................. 112

Jasper ................................................................... 113

Kyanite ................................................................. 116

Labradorite ........................................................... 117

Lapis Lazuli ........................................................... 118

Lepidolite ............................................................. 120

Malachite ............................................................. 122

Moonstone ........................................................... 124

Obsidian ............................................................... 125

Onyx ..................................................................... 128

- Petrified Wood .......... 129
- Prehnite .......... 130
- Quartz .......... 131
- Rhodochrosite .......... 134
- Rhodonite .......... 135
- Ruby .......... 136
- Sodalite .......... 137
- Sugilite .......... 138
- Sunstone .......... 139
- Tiger's Eye .......... 140
- Tigers Iron .......... 142
- Topaz .......... 143
- Unakite .......... 145

## Angels, spirit guides and ascended masters .......... 148
- Angels .......... 148
  - Archangel List .......... 150
    - List of the archangels, their associated crystals and what areas they cover .......... 158
- Spirit guides .......... 160
- Ascended masters .......... 162

## Colour Therapy .......... 165
- So what exactly is colour? .......... 165
  - Colour wheel .......... 167
- Characteristics of the colours .......... 168
  - Red .......... 169
  - Orange .......... 169

    Yellow .................................................................. 170

    Green .................................................................. 171

    Pale Blue ............................................................. 172

    Indigo .................................................................. 172

    Violet .................................................................. 173

    Other colours of interest in healing. .............. 173

How to use colour in your life for healing. ................. 175

    Wearing colour ................................................. 175

    Using coloured water ...................................... 176

    Colour table for physical dis-ease ................. 178

    Coloured silks ................................................... 179

    Colour breathing .............................................. 179

    Meditating with colour ................................... 182

    Visualisation with colour ................................. 185

    Eating colour .................................................... 188

Altars .............................................................................. 193

    Altar examples ................................................. 202

Meditation ..................................................................... 213

    Specific meditations for specific healings... ... 216

Visualisation .................................................................. 228

Gratitude. ....................................................................... 236

Well my friends ............................................................. 238

INDEX .............................................................................. 241

# My Journey

The challenges started when I began to travel my spiritual pathway. My first experience of anything spiritual came when my mother-in-law took me to a healing circle. She had been going for a while and thought I might find it helpful because I had suffered eczema on the palms of my hands for many years. At the time they were giving me a lot of problems. I was excited as I walked in and sat down in a chair to receive my healing. I remember a wonderful feeling of relaxation flowing through me as I drifted off to I don't know where.

I remember the lady placing her hands on my shoulders and gently asking me to come back and open my eyes. I jumped with a start because I'd thought it was she who had been holding my feet firmly! As I opened my eyes I looked to my ankles but nobody at all was holding them there. She just smiled and said my guide had been assisting her with the healing. Then I was curious and asked what she meant about 'my guide' assisting her. She explained that we all have spirit guides who help us from above and went on to say that I would become a very powerful healer.

I laughed as I thanked her and said I knew nothing about healing or spirit guides, but the feeling was so wonderful that I continued to go each week. Soon I began to become involved in learning how to feel the energies around people. It was an amazing time. I began to read various spiritual books and became interested in crystals. My (now) ex at first was very supportive and listened as I droned on and on about how wonderful the people were and how wonderful I was feeling. I totally immersed myself in my new found world.

This was the first of my challenges. He started to say I was changing – that I no longer loved him and was obsessed by my new friends. I tried hard to involve him but he had no real interest. After several months as our relationship broke down he finally said it was him or them. So, reluctantly, I gave up my involvement with friends and devoted myself to him.

Soon, the patter of little feet helped me to forget my loss as I devoted myself to our son. I have to say 'loss' because that was how it felt. It was as if a large part of me had been taken away. I was denying who I truly was. By that time, we were living in Germany, going back to England to visit his family every couple of years. It was one such visit that changed my life again. We went into a book store where he went to look at autobiographies while I went to the cookery section. Having chosen a book, I drifted to other shelves and soon found myself reaching for one about Angels and Spirit guides. It felt as though a force had taken me there. I looked at the book with shock and quickly looked over my shoulder. Luckily my ex was nowhere to be seen.

I knew the book was for me and had to have it, but it was a huge risk. My interest in spiritual things had nearly ended my marriage before and I knew, if he found the book, it would cause no end of problems. I remember walking to the counter, praying he wouldn't see me and he didn't. I smuggled the book back home and used to wait for him to leave for work before immersing myself in the book when my son was sleeping. That book changed my life and started me on the greatest journey of my life. It opened up something inside me that had lain dormant for too many years. Yes, my journey had truly begun.

I continued to buy more books secretly, expanding my knowledge. Every time I needed help to reach the next level I was guided to the right book or person. I was very happy with my son but the relationship with my husband was strained. My parents picked up on it but never interfered. We moved again, this time to Spain and soon my daughter came along. Our relationship was once again strengthened as she was born at twenty-seven weeks weighing only 940grams and we both dedicated ourselves to her survival. My time was fully consumed, looking after my two children.

Slowly, as the children grew, I was once again drawn back to books and my spiritual life, into which came new friends. I felt happy: told myself I was very blessed. After all I had everything I could possibly need but, deep inside, I knew I didn't love my husband any more. He was controlling and would fly off the handle if things were not to his taste. I thought, having made my bed, I must lie in it. I couldn't upset the children and was too scared of my husband to leave him.

Having not worked for many years I knew only how to be a wife and mother. My self-esteem was very low and I lacked confidence. I didn't speak Spanish well so my chance of getting a job was low. On the odd occasions when work found me, my ex-husband always undermined my enthusiasm. *'We don't need the money, they are taking advantage of you, they are not paying you what you are worth'* …these words were drilled into me until I thought he was right and I would leave.

Then he was happy, knowing I was at home being a housewife! I didn't realise at the time that he had control issues and needed to know exactly where I was, all the time. He also had insecurity issues because he asked if there were men where I worked and if they spoke to me! If there were, he warned me to be careful and avoid them in case they got the wrong idea. I never questioned what he meant but obeyed, saying no more than hello to them and getting on with my work.

I found comfort in spiritual pursuits. My ex mother-in-law

was very involved in the spiritual side of life and had begun to do automatic writing. This is where someone relaxes and allows the spirit world to pass information on, via the instrument they hold. Their hand is guided to put words on paper. She used to tell me about her writings and said that one day I would write like her. I waited for such a day. Time passed and I accepted my lot.

One year, friends from Mallorca came to visit. We hadn't seen them for some years. They came for a week and stayed with us at my parent's house, which, at the time, we were house sitting. For me it was wonderful because we touched briefly on spiritual things. My husband was not happy at all, he would have preferred to drink as in the old days but they were not interested. He was happy when they left – they were boring, he said, and no fun anymore. Disagreeing with him was a mistake and we had a huge row.

Knowing it was the safest thing to do, because he'd been drinking, I went to bed and woke in the early hours of the morning to find the television blaring, doors wide open and lights left on. I didn't see him so assumed he had fallen asleep by the pool area. In the morning I realised our car had gone. I guessed he had driven home in the night and then worried as he had been drinking heavily. When the phone rang shrilly, I knew it was him. I answered and was shocked to hear a cold voice asking to speak to the children. There was no apology or explanation ...nothing but a cold voice and a very negative energy came to me. It shook me to the core and I had to accept that I was truly in a dead end marriage. That night after putting the kids to bed I sat in a chair and asked for spirit guidance. I closed my eyes, letting the tears fall and, drifting into a meditative state, asked if there was anybody there; *I needed help now!* A voice said "how can I help you my child".

I remember thinking, *oh no, not only am I in a dead end*

*marriage but now I have gone mad – I'm hearing voices in my head.* The voice laughed, and then said no I wasn't mad. I opened my eyes panic-stricken expecting to see someone standing in the room. I was ready to run for my life, thinking a burglar had entered the house! There was no one there. The voice was so real I was convinced someone was there and even ended up looking inside cupboards to check! This was the start of my most magical journey. I spoke to the voice for what seemed like minutes but in fact was two hours. I asked all sorts of questions about myself, my husband, everything that I needed guidance on. Afterwards, I wrote everything down so I would not forget. This was when I realised I was clairaudient. I could 'hear' what spirit was saying. So I wasn't going mad…that was a big relief!

My channelling continued and brought me much guidance. I continued in the relationship with my husband but knew that, when the time was right, I would find the courage to leave. One morning I was surprised to find my husband's car outside the house after I had dropped the children off at school. He would normally have been at work by that time. I entered the house with a sinking feeling knowing something was wrong. Being very sensitive to energies by now I could feel the heaviness around the house. I was right to feel it because the first thing I saw when I entered the lounge were my spiritual books and angel oracle cards strewn across the table. My books and cards had been in my book cupboard for years and he had never questioned their presence. I felt immense anger with him for touching my things in such a way. He launched into a verbal attack about how I had deceived him by having such books in the house.

Calmly collecting my stuff to put it away, I stated that the books had been there for years and, if he didn't like it, tough. He stormed off only to return hours later to state that it was him or the books. Knowing it was time to stand up for my beliefs, I told him the suitcase was in the wardrobe. I remember trembling inside but was determined not to show fear – even asking the angels to help shield me and give me the courage that would be needed to end things with him.

It was only the beginning of a long challenging pathway that helped me to grow to a level that hadn't seemed possible. Leaving him and getting divorced, took three years and huge amounts of tears and pain, but I made it through and can now look back and smile at it. If someone had told me what I would have to go through I would have laughed and told them– that kind of thing only happened in movies, not in real life! Surely, nobody would put someone through such suffering after they had been married for twenty-one years, but I was wrong. He did put me through the mill and then some, but we have an amazing amount of strength inside us; we just need to believe in it. When we do we can accomplish anything we set out to do.

I still have lessons to learn but for me the worst is behind me and now I KNOW I can face any challenge thrown my way!

So, you see, I know the journey, for we all have to tread it on our pathway of ascension. All that needs to be cleared from this life and past lives must be faced and dealt with. At times you may think you will never make it and are being punished for some forgotten sin you must have committed. You are not being punished, you are being guided to become the best that you can be. We are never given more than we can handle. The old saying, 'What doesn't kill us makes us stronger!' is so true. We always find a way. We draw on that hidden inner strength. So embrace life and its myriad of challenges and know that we truly are blessed to be here. Use this book with my blessings and I hope it helps you on your pathway.

# Part 1
# Understanding what we are…

# The building blocks of life

The human body is comprised of more than a hundred million cells. These cells are microscopic and vary in shape and size, according to the function they have to do. Some cells are used for muscles and these have to be long and thin so they can contract and relax. While others such as the liver cells, are hexagonal in shape as they have to carry out a multitude of chemical processes. Despite there being variations in the size and shape of cells within the body, they are all constructed according to the same basic pattern. They are comprised of atoms. These atoms contain electrons, protons and neutrons. Electrons carry a negative electrical charge, protons a positive electrical charge, while neutrons have no electrical charge.

Scientists once believed that these were the smallest particles to be found in existence but this theory was replaced when quantum physicists discovered that the atoms could be broken down into even smaller parts. These physicists discovered that the smallest particles were actually vibrating masses of energy, which as such could not be quantified into an exact measurement. Each 'particle' of energy blended with the next without any definitive end.

This was a huge breakthrough in the science world and in the 'holistic' world because at last there was proof that we, as humans, are comprised of energy. A fact that the 'holistic' world has been saying for years! This proof brought significant changes; people began to realise that they had control over their health. That they could heal themselves using more natural ingredients than those prescribed by doctors.

Each body cell vibrates at a different frequency. This is how the different structures of the body are formed, such as the organs, nerves, blood, skeleton etc. Each structure when vibrating at its optimum frequency will result in perfect health. However, when the structures are vibrating at the wrong frequency, ill health will result in that structure, be it the liver, kidney or a muscle etc. In order to return the structure to perfect health the imbalance of energy needs to be returned to its correct frequency. Quantum physicists carried out various experiments on the 'energy' and found that the protons, electrons and neutrons didn't necessarily move as they were supposed to. In fact, they became very erratic in their behaviour at times before settling into a more controlled reaction.

Many experiments were carried out to see if different scientists observed the same things. Each experiment was carried out under strictly controlled conditions but the results varied. The only 'uncontrolled' aspect of the experiment was the scientist conducting it. The only explanation was that the scientists could control the experiments by their thoughts. This theory was tested and found to be true. The energy could be controlled by mere 'thought' alone. This opened the way for holistic therapists to prove that we are the cause of our own ill health. A view point that has been discounted by doctors for many years.

As 'energy' we can control our own health; because energy will move and react according to the programme that it is given. Or put another way, it can be controlled by our thoughts. This is why some people who strongly believe they are going to overcome life threatening illnesses usually do. Why, otherwise, is someone cured by a 'placebo' or sugar pill? It is not the pill that cures the illness but the person's 'thought programme' – their strong belief that the pill will cure. If you believe in it, then it will. Many people have experienced this. There have been cases where an illness has returned, because belief in them was lost after the patient was told that the pills were only sugar and had not cured anything.

The mind is an incredible piece of equipment and we are only just beginning to realise just how powerful it is. It is interesting to note that we don't have to have total belief that 'we' can heal ourselves, as long as we have a belief that someone else can heal us. This is how many miracle workers 'heal'. If someone believes strongly that another person can heal them, then they can be. Healers or holistic therapists can balance the energies in the body but the recipient must have some belief that the treatment will work for the healing to be permanent.

Alternatively, they need to have discovered the root cause of the problem during the treatment. A person's energy imbalances can be balanced and they will go away feeling fine for a while but if they don't believe they are being helped on a deeper level, or the root cause hasn't been released, then the imbalance will reoccur. The root cause of a problem needs to be released for the energies to stay in balance; eventually, if not, a symptom will appear again.

We now know that we consist of energy. We are in fact a large vibrating mass of it. We also know that energy, as such, has no boundary to it. It flows from one vibrating particle into the next. So even though we see our body as having a distinct shape or outline, our energy still flows out from the part where the skin contains our body. This is how the aura is formed. It is a 'luminous' glow, which emanates from all living matter radiating out beyond the physical realm that is made up of different vibrations or frequencies. It is also referred to as our subtle energy field or our electromagnetic energy field. In its simplest terms it is a continuation of the energy field of our body.

This is where scientific meets spiritual! The body you now

know is made of energy and this energy has no finish. The next chapter will explain in more detail what the aura is and how it functions in relation to the physical body.

# The aura and chakra systems

The aura is also referred to as the bio-magnetic field. It surrounds the body and extends out several feet. It can be divided into seven layers. These are the layers that I pick up as a healer. Each layer has a slightly different feel to it. My belief is that as you move 'up' the layers, away from the body the frequency increases to a higher level. This is supported by many other healers. The lowest layer is much denser and is therefore much easier to detect, while the upper layers are more difficult to perceive. Their vibration is so fine that it takes practice to be able to discern between the layers. This distinction between the layers is not vital as healing will still occur. It is only useful when a healer wants to trace the root cause of a problem: emotional, mental, present or past life. Within the aura there is a series of energy centres called chakras. These energy centres work directly with the aura and the physical body.

The chakras are thought to vitalize the physical body and to be associated with interactions of a physical, emotional and mental nature. They ascend upwards from the base of the spine to the top of the head, and extend out from the physical body and up through the aura. They are cone-like in appearance, drawing energy from all around us directly into the body. They can be likened to little power stations dotted all over the body.

There are seven main chakras and twenty-one minor chakras. The seven main chakras are linked to the seven layers of the aura. These chakras, in turn, are linked to the seven glands of the endocrine system. We can now see, beginning to form, a correlation between the energy systems and the physical body, from a scientific point of view.

The name chakra is derived from the Sanskrit word for wheel or turning. Many different cultures refer to the chakra system in their healing systems. They are considered to be the loci of life energy or prana, also called Shakti (Chinese), qi (Japanese), Koach-ha-guf (Hebrew), bios (Greek) & aether (Greek, English).

The function of the chakras is to spin and draw in this energy to keep the spiritual, mental, emotional and physical health of the body in balance. They are said by some to reflect how the unified consciousness of humanity (the immortal human being or the soul), is divided to manage different aspects of earthly life (body instinct, vital energy, deeper emotions, communication, having an overview of life, contact to God).

# The seven main chakras and their locations

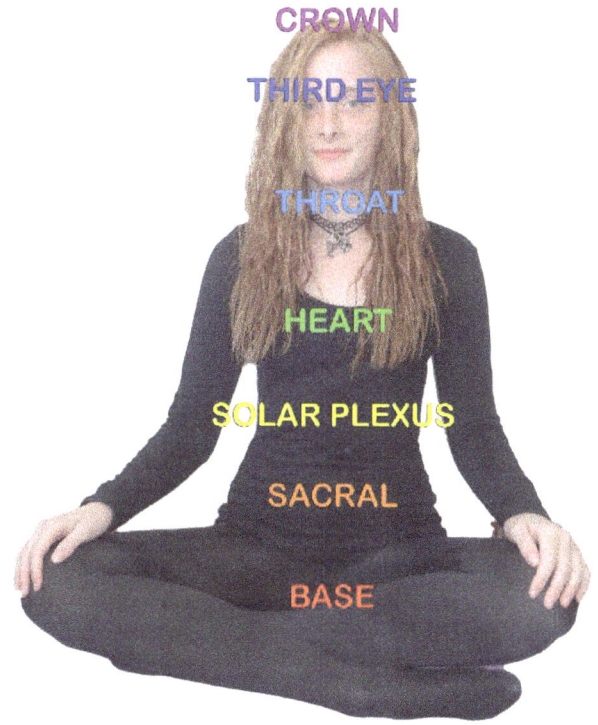

Let us now begin to explore the seven layers of the aura and their link to the seven main chakras.

## The first layer or Etheric Body

This is a replica of the physical body. It extends outward from the physical body 0.5-4cm. The chakra that channels the energy through this layer takes on the same colour. This layer can appear as a pulsing wave that moves over the body or it may feel much denser than the other layers of the aura. In this layer it is easier to feel any areas of blocked energy. The blockages will directly correspond to any problems within the physical body. For example, if the liver is 'stressed' it will be felt as an area of stagnant energy in the etheric layer, exactly over the site of the liver in the physical body, but it will be 0.5-4cm above the body. When we experience strong emotions or stressful situations they cause an imbalance in the etheric layer. This will cause an immediate energy imbalance.

At first it will only cause an imbalance in the etheric layer and there will be no lasting effects felt in the physical body. However, if the imbalance continues for long enough, the physical body will start to show symptoms of this imbalance. At first the symptoms will be slight but, if the problem remains unresolved, then the symptoms will get worse. As the energy imbalance continues it will start to show in other layers of the aura too.

If it is emotionally based, it will show in the second layer; if it is mentally based it will show in the third layer. When I conduct a healing session I always take note of any areas of stagnation, whether the client has said there is a problem in the area or not. All problems will primarily show in this layer before they show in the physical body. In some cases, problems can be resolved and cleared before they even manifest in the physical body. This is a good example of where a 'maintenance' treatment programme can be useful! A monthly maintenance treatment could help work as a deterrent for any problems occurring.

## The second layer or the Emotional Body

This layer is associated with our feelings. It is where we 'hold' our emotions. It can be felt as a lovely 'smooth' energy or as a 'turbulent' energy, depending again on the feelings that the client is experiencing at the time. When a client is excited, joyful or in love, for example, the energy will feel smooth and vibrant but if the client is going through a difficult time and is very stressed, then the energy will be lumpy and heavy to the touch. When our feelings are very positive (such as love and joy etc.) the colours will appear bright; if feelings are confused or stressed they will appear murky or dull.

This layer extends out from the body from 2-6cm. Imbalances of energy coming from the etheric layer will show in this area if they are formed from an emotional basis.

As third dimension colours, the chakras in this layer traditionally take on the colours stated below:

$1^{st}$ chakra or base, RED

$2^{nd}$ chakra or sacral, ORANGE

$3^{rd}$ chakra or solar plexus, YELLOW

$4^{th}$ chakra or heart, GREEN

$5^{th}$ chakra or throat, PALE BLUE

$6^{th}$ chakra or brow or third eye, INDIGO

$7^{th}$ chakra or crown, WHITE

These colours were originally perceived when the planet, Mother Earth, was in a denser dimension leading up to the end of 2012. This was the date foreseen by the Mayans, who were a highly spiritually-evolved tribe, as being the end of Planet Earth. They wrote calendars, depicting what would happen to the world, which went only as far as 21-12-12. Many people believed this to mean that it would be the end of the planet but, as we now know, it wasn't! They only chose it because they knew that, after 2012, the Planet's energies or frequencies would change. They were unable to foresee how Mother Earth, or we as a race, would react to the energy changes. The earth could have reacted with massive natural disasters, resulting in huge loss of life but, luckily for us, a gentler approach was taken.

Yet many of us felt that 'something' was happening inside, we sensed uneasiness: a feeling of being unsettled or restless. Our jobs, which once fulfilled us, were now unsatisfactory. Our relationships, which we had thought were ok, were becoming unglued and showing huge gaps that we couldn't cross. Many people changed their careers, their partners and even how they lived. This deep unease brought about huge changes to some people. These changes are still being felt by some. Massive emotional clearings are going on with people.

All those stored-up emotions are surfacing to be faced and cleared. So is it any wonder that people are feeling out of balance. Our bodies have taken a massive upheaval in this life time. The planet has changed to a higher frequency and caused our frequencies to change. We have evolved to a higher frequency, which doesn't allow emotions or traumas to be held in the body …all will come out now, to be released. Whereas we were once like stained tablecloths in a darkened room, seemingly perfect, we now have light shining on us, showing up all those emotional 'stains'.

We are realising that we are not as unblemished as we thought but fear not, we can clear these emotions and become brilliant white again!

When, as souls, we evolve to higher frequencies or dimensions, the chakras begin to move from their positions in the body, downwards towards the legs, to allow the new, higher, chakras to enter. These operate at the new, higher frequencies. They bring us into alignment with the higher frequencies of the planet. The chakras' colours will change as we bring in the higher frequencies.

These new colours will not be seen by many but some might feel them. When healing someone one can always tell the more highly evolved souls, as they have a very different energy. For me it is a knowing rather than a seeing! I have always been sensitive to feeling things. The moment someone with a powerful energy walks into a room, people feel compelled to turn and look at them because their presence is felt. Most of us have these feelings but few trust and use them. They are gifts bestowed upon us but, sadly, too few use them.

## The third layer or the Mental Body

This layer deals with our mental chatter. It processes our thoughts and our mental reasoning. This layer can be felt as either active energy, when a person has many mental processes going on, or a gentler energy when the person is at peace with little mental chatter. This layer extends out from the body from 6-16cm. Our ideas are formed in this level.

When our ideas are in full flow and we are actively thinking, then the energy in this layer can be very active and lively. However, when we are weighed down by our mental chatter and are unable to process our ideas, the energy will be very sluggish.

This layer works in conjunction with the second layer because we hold emotional feelings to our ideas as well.

Distinguishing between these layers can be more difficult but our intuition can help us to distinguish where the problem originates. Sometimes, healing the emotional issues attached to a problem, can result in clarity in the mental body, which will enable us to find the solution to carry our mental ideas onward to fruition; and vice versa. Clearing a mental block can release our feelings in the emotional body. So it can be said that these two layers work closely together at times.

These first three layers are very much associated with the physical world. These layers metabolise the energies that directly affect the physical body. When working on the lower three layers, any imbalances felt will show in the physical body. They are what I call surface disturbances. They are easier to detect and easier to resolve because they are a direct consequence of issues that have occurred in our present life.

## The fourth layer or Astral Level

This layer resembles closely the emotional layer. It is the bridge between the physical layers and the spiritual layers. It extends from 15-30 cm from the body. This layer is what I call the cording layer. It is where we make our connections with other people on an energetic level. It is the level where we build connections of energy that connect to another's aura.

Where our connections of energy (cords, as they are otherwise known) connect will depend on the type of relationship we have with that person. If we are with a person for our 'survival' (in the sense that they provide a roof etc. over our head) then we will start to make connections to the base chakra. Purely sexual connections will cord at the sacral chakra.

If we have an intellectual relationship with someone then the cords may connect at our solar plexus. Love relationships will connect directly at the heart chakra. Family and close friends will always have a cord attached to the heart centres. These cords are beneficial to both parties. They give us that feeling of connection. The cords are attached to the front of the body in healthy relationships.

When a relationship has run its course and is no longer required by one party the connection will be severed. However, when the opposite party is not in agreement to the ending of the relationship they can send out cords that latch on to the chakras on the back of the body. We are often unaware of this as it is done on an energetic level, but we will sense that the other person just won't let go of us. We may feel emotionally drained and physically drained. We will think of the other person and find it hard to clear them from our thoughts. This is because they are very much still connected to us. These cords are unhealthy and will need to be cut. This can be done by a technique called cord cutting meditation, covered later in the book.

## The fifth or Etheric Template Body

This layer is a template for the physical body. It is a bit like a negative of a photograph. It is a blueprint of how our physical body should look. It extends from 45- 60cm from the body. This is the first of the spiritual levels and provides a template for the etheric layer of the physical body to work from. When healers work at this level they can assist in rebalancing the etheric level of the first layer. Past-life injuries are held in this layer. If these injuries were never processed during the life time in which they occurred, then the trauma will carry over into the next life. It will continue to do so until we have learned the lessons we needed to learn from the injury. The trauma will remain in the fifth layer and cause problems in our present life.

Illnesses that just won't clear or for which the medical profession cannot find a reason, are often past-life traumas. Most often there is no injury or problem to be found at the site of the pain, which is why many doctors will send people away saying it's all in their head! There won't be an injury because it is merely an energetic blockage being carried forward from a past life. Often when I work on this layer I see how the person sustained the injury. Most often the wounds will be putrid in appearance. Usually, the angels (discussed later in the book) assist me in clearing out the 'gunk' and they fill the area with divine light.

The person usually feels an immediate release of some kind. They feel lighter as if a weight has been taken off their shoulders. Once the trauma has been cleared work on the other layers can begin to bring balance to the whole body.

## The sixth or the Celestial Body

This layer is the emotional body of the spiritual level. It extends 60- 80cm from the body. It is the layer where past life emotional traumas are held. It is similar to the last layer where past life traumas are retained from emotions that have not been dealt with in previous lives and will have an impact upon this life. Past lives where we were hurt by bad relationships can have an impact upon current relationships. We may feel it hard to trust a romantic partner but be unsure why, because we have not had any hurtful breakups. Lives where we lost many loved ones may affect us in this life by preventing us from wanting to get close to another person, in case we lose them too. If we were sexually abused in past lives, we may have problems with sex in this life but not understand why.

These emotions are very powerful and will be carried with us until we learn from their origin. During healing, these emotions can be cleared and the person helped to understand why they existed. Once the reason has been located the emotions attached to it can be dealt with by the sufferer. As the emotions are from past lives they can be dealt with easily from a detached point of view. As they are not from this life, it can feel as if you are working on someone else when you start to unveil these emotions.

I had a lot of pent-up emotions from back in the time of Atlantis. I was unaware of the emotions being there until I bought myself a rather beautiful quartz trigonic point. The first time I meditated with it I had an incredible surge of sadness well up in me. I remember thinking what on earth is all this about! I stayed with the feeling and the quartz revealed the start of the fall of Atlantis. I had all the emotions running through me and I was crying profusely but it was like I was someone else. It didn't have the same feeling to it as a current emotional reaction would. It was a very powerful release for me and I felt relief afterwards as if a huge weight had been lifted.

## The seventh or Causal Body

This is the mental level of the spiritual body. It extends from 75-100cm from the body. This is the level that contains all the information that we need for our lessons in this lifetime. It is our map of this life. It is what we have decided to learn, to experience and to express now, from a purely spiritual aspect. It is the last level that one can perceive in a human body.
Each of these layers draws in universal energy and filters it down towards the physical body. The chakras of the etheric

layer filter the energy directly into the endocrine glands that are connected to each chakra. These glands then process the energy and use it in their various bodily functions.

This is just an overview of what the different layers of the aura do. Healers will work directly with these layers but on your healing pathway you will be unable to feel the different layers due to the fact that they extend out too far. You may 'feel' where the problem lies, using your intuition, or find a trusted healer who can guide you to the areas that need work.

# The seven main chakras

Our chakras rotate in a clockwise fashion as they draw in the universal energy. When they are functioning to the optimum we will feel lively and vibrant. Life will be fun and exciting. We will look forward eagerly to each new day and then embrace it wholeheartedly. Everything will flow easily in our life. Doors will constantly open with new opportunities to add to our experiences. In short, we will feel ecstatic to be alive.

    This is a state of being, however, that we only tend to view at certain times in our life. We can wake up one morning feeling wonderful only to wake up the next day feeling blue! This occurs when one, or more, of our chakras is not rotating correctly. It might be rotating too fast, too slow or be blocked. Our lives are full of many challenges and these challenges can affect our chakras, causing them to spin incorrectly. Let's take a look at the seven main chakras and their connection to the physical body.

*First: Base chakra*

*Second: Sacral chakra*

*Third: Solar plexus chakra*

*Fourth: Heart chakra*

*Fifth: Throat chakra*

*Sixth: Third eye chakra*

*Seventh: Crown chakra*

## Base Chakra

Muladhara or root chakra is symbolized by a lotus with four petals. The base chakra governs our instincts, security, survival and our potentiality. Physically, it is connected to our sexuality, mentally to our stability, emotionally our sensuality, and spiritually our sense of security. It is connected to the sense of smell. This first chakra is at the base of the spine. It is concerned with our physical needs and basic human survival and controls the automatic and autonomic functioning of the physical body.

This centre nourishes and governs the Spinal column, skeletal structure and the kidneys. It works with the endocrine system via the adrenal glands. These glands are situated above the kidneys. They sit one on each kidney like a cap. Each gland has two distinct parts: the inner medulla and the outer covering, called the cortex. Both secrete hormones.

## Sacral Chakra

Swadhisthana is the other name given to the sacral chakra. It is symbolized by a lotus within which is a crescent moon, with six vermillion, or orange petals. This chakra is involved with our relationships (both with our self and others), violent tendencies, addictions, our emotional needs, and pleasure. Physically, it governs reproduction. Mentally it governs creativity. Emotionally it governs joy and spiritually it governs enthusiasm.

The second chakra is located just below the navel. It governs our emotional aspects. We feel our emotions through this centre. It is our joy centre, through which we express whatever we create in life. We are all artists of life. We may not be painters or musicians but we all use our creative abilities every day to prepare food, get dressed, take care of our houses or bring a child into this world. These are all acts of creation, which are felt and processed in this centre. Our sexuality is also a part of its functioning.

How we relate to our sexuality is important because it is a part of us whether we express it or not. When we experience sex with someone we are in love with, all centres will be involved and the feelings of joy will be expressed at their most powerful. The experience of orgasm is the closest that we can feel to the oneness of creation. However, we must not restrict ourselves to the sexual form alone, but must connect to our inner child and learn to 'play'. When we play we release the energy of joy. When children play they release huge amounts of joy energy which we hear as giggling. This is a good yardstick to apply to how much joy we feel in life. When something makes us laugh out loud, we know we are releasing joy energy.

The sacral centre is connected to the endocrine system via the gonads. It nourishes and governs the reproductive system. The gonads are represented in the male by the testes and in the female by the ovaries.

## Solar Plexus Chakra

Manipura is the other name given to the solar plexus and it is symbolized by a downward pointing triangle with ten petals. This centre governs our personal power, fear, anxiety, opinions, introversion, and transition from simple emotions to more complex. Physically, it governs digestion, mentally it governs personal power, emotionally it governs expansiveness, and spiritually, all matters of spiritual growth. This third chakra controls all our mental aspects and linear thinking. It governs our relationship with our self.

The centre is located just below the diaphragm. This centre nourishes and governs the liver and gall bladder, nervous system and stomach and is connected to the endocrine system via the pancreas.

# Heart Chakra

Anahata, or Anahata-puri, or padma-sundara, are the names that are also associated with the heart chakra. It is represented by a circular flower with twelve green petals. Within it are two intersecting triangles, forming a hexagram, symbolising a union of the male and female. This centre is associated with complex emotions, compassion, tenderness, unconditional love, equilibrium, rejection and well-being.

Physically this centre governs circulation. Emotionally it governs unconditional love for oneself and others. Mentally it governs passion, and spiritually it governs devotion.

The centre is found in the midpoint of the chest. It is connected to the endocrine system via the thymus gland. This centre nourishes and governs the heart, blood, vagus nerve and the circulatory system.

The thymus is found in the upper part of the chest, just behind the breast bone.

## Throat Chakra

Vishuddha (also Vishuddhi) is the other name associated with the throat chakra. It is depicted as a silver crescent within a white circle, with 16 light or pale blue or turquoise petals. The fifth chakra is associated with all forms of communication and how we connect to the world. 'Speaking', listening, being and taking responsibility for our actions. It is the link between how we communicate and our emotional expression of the heart centre. Physically, this chakra governs communication. Emotionally it governs independence. Mentally it governs fluent thought and, spiritually, it governs a sense of security.

The centre is located in the throat area and it nourishes and governs the bronchial and vocal apparatus, lungs and alimentary canal. It is connected to the endocrine system via the thyroid and parathyroid gland. The thyroid gland is situated in the neck just below the larynx.

# Third Eye Chakra

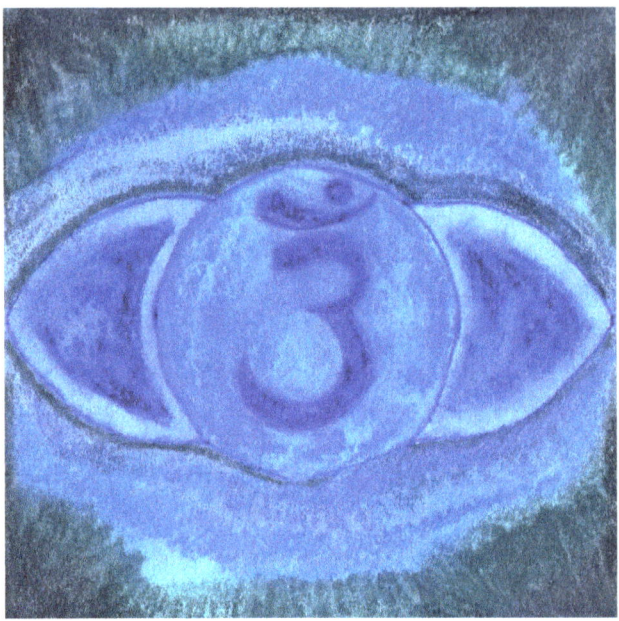

Ajna is the other name by which the third eye or brow chakra is known. It is symbolized by a lotus with two petals. The two petals are thought to represent the ending of duality. It is the merging of our physical body with our spiritual body so we are at oneness with all that exists. This sixth chakra is associated with our connection to the divine, celestial love. It is the centre that shows us that we are all inter-connected; we are all one: a divine manifestation. It deals with balancing the higher and lower selves and trusting inner guidance. This chakra relates to the access of intuition. Mentally, it deals with visual consciousness. Emotionally, it deals with clarity on an intuitive level.

Located between the eyebrows this centre is connected to the endocrine system by the pituitary gland. This centre nourishes and governs the nose, left eye, ears, lower brain and nervous system.

# Crown Chakra

Sahasrara is the other name by which the crown chakra is known.

It means the thousand petalled lotus. This is the chakra of pure consciousness. It is associated with the higher mind, our knowing and intuitive spiritual side. It is located on the top of the head. It is connected to the endocrine system via the pineal gland. This centre nourishes and governs the right eye and upper brain. Little is fully understood about the pineal gland but it is thought to play a role in the body's circadian rhythms. This is the twenty-four-hour rhythm of lightness and dark which the body relates to. As you can begin to see, there is a direct connection between the spiritual centres (chakras) and the main glands of the body. Each system works directly with the other to bring perfect health to the body. As well as the main seven chakras, which work directly with the endocrine glands, there are minor chakras that deal with other issues in the body.

# The Major Chakras and their associations in the body.

| CHAKRA | LOCATION | ENDOCRINE GLAND | BODY AREA |
|---|---|---|---|
| **Base** | Base of spine | Adrenal glands | Bones, skeletal structure, kidneys |
| **Sacral** | Behind navel | Reproductive organs | Reproductive organs, bladder, circulatory system, prostate, womb |
| **Solar Plexus** | Base of sternum | Pancreas | Digestive system, muscles, liver, gall bladder, nervous system |
| **Heart** | Centre of chest | Thymus | Heart, chest, lungs, circulation |
| **Throat** | Throat | Thyroid | Throat, ears, teeth, mouth, neck, vocal apparatus |
| **Third Eye** | Between the eyebrows | Pituitary gland | Eyes, base of skull, nervous system, nose |
| **Crown** | Top of head | Pineal gland | Upper skull, cerebral cortex, skin |

# The Lower Chakras

There are seven smaller chakras located in the legs. These are thought to deal with our base animal instincts.

They are the:

**Atala:** These chakras are located in the hip area. They are concerned with our fears and sexual desires. The opposing attribute, to balance them, is governed by the right to be sexual: to be able to feel completely comfortable with who you are and your sexual preferences.

**Vitala**: These chakras are located in the thighs. They are concerned with our issues of anger and resentment. The opposing attribute, to balance this chakra, is forgiveness. We must be able to forgive ourselves as well as others. We are all a divine spark of pure light and, as such, are all equal. When we perceive others as doing wrong to us it is generally the universe showing us an aspect of ourselves that we have not mastered and brought under control.

This aspect will keep being mirrored in us until we master it. Forgiveness is about being able to see that another has acted from their belief systems, however evolved or not they are. Many confuse forgiveness with accepting that others who have wronged you were right to have done so. This is not the case. We can forgive someone without accepting or agreeing that what they did was right. We just have to acknowledge that, at that time, for whatever reason, they acted in the way they did.

**Sutala**: These chakras are located in the knees. They are concerned with jealousy. When we are not confident with who we are we look to others and perceive them as being better. This often brings up deep-seated emotions and feelings of inadequacy. These can be from a current life experience, or from a past life experience. The opposing attribute, to balance this chakra, is the right to be self-confident, to accept whatever we are with confidence.

**Talatala**: These chakras are located in the calves. They govern our animal instincts and our will to react to them. The opposing attribute, to balance this chakra, is the right to be conscious. To be happy and to react consciously to what our body is telling us. We so often ignore what our bodies tell us. When we do this repeatedly our body will find a way to make us listen. This is usually by giving us an illness that will knock us off our feet for a few days! This way, the body has time to sort out what it needs, knowing that we can't resist!!

**Rasatala**: These chakras are located in the ankles. They govern the centre of selfishness and pure animal nature. We need to find the balance for this chakra because we tend to fall into one category or the other. We are either inherently selfish thinking only of ourselves, or inherently charitable and thinking only of others. We need to find a balance between giving and accepting. These deep set patterns of selfishness or excessive giving are usually set up from an early age according to how our parents etc. were brought up. This unfortunately can become a deep-seated pattern that stays with us for life. It sets up an immediate imbalance because we have to be able to give and receive equally.

We need to have this balance in our life. When we only give (denying others the pleasure of helping us), or when we only take (never experiencing the joy of helping), we are creating a build-up of negative energy. This negative energy will stay in and around the aura creating blockages, which will impede the flow of energy through the chakras. We will eventually become depleted of energy and then will not be able to help anyone, including ourselves! The opposing attribute, to balance this chakra, is finding the balance of giving and taking and experiencing the joy that both give.

**Mahatala and Patala**: These chakras are located in the soles of the feet. These are the chakras that are in contact with mother Earth. They lead us blindly forward through life. We never consciously see what is below them as we step forward through life. When we are on our correct pathway in life, we step forward fearlessly into the unknown knowing that these chakras will lead us. When they are out of balance we falter in our steps. We question our direction in life. So follow your pathway with confidence.

The chart sums up the chakras and their corresponding connection to the endocrine glands. When we experience disease (disease) in the body, look to the chakra associated with it to find the area that you need to work on. Each chakra covers various organs and areas with its energetic connections, so if one of these areas is out of sync, by working on the chakra directly, you can start to clear the energetic blockage.

# Chart showing the minor chakras and their associations in the body.

| CHAKRA | LOCATION | NEGATIVE ATTRIBUTES | POSITIVE ATTRIBUTES |
|---|---|---|---|
| **Atala** | Hip area | Our fears and sexual desires | Feeling comfortable with who we are and our sexuality |
| **Vitala** | Thighs | Issues of anger and resentment | Forgiveness of the self and others |
| **Sutala** | Knees | Jealousy | Self confidence |
| **Talatala** | Calves | Our animal instincts and our will to react | To be happy and to react consciously |
| **Rasatala** | Ankles | Selfishness or charitable to excess | To find the balance of giving and taking |
| **Mahatala and Patala** | Feet and soles of feet | Inability to walk our path in life without faltering | Connecting with Mother earth and to walk our path with confidence |

## Additional chakras

As well as the major seven chakras and the minor chakras there are four additional chakras.

**Earth chakra:** This is located below the feet. It grounds us on the earth plane. It is our 'earthly' connection. When this centre is balanced we feel connected to our earthly life. We exist in the 'here and now'. It is our centre of reality. It is our centre of empowerment. It enables us to accept that we are a soul living an earthly existence. This is felt on a soul level. When this centre is blocked then we feel out of sync. It is usually felt as a physical discomfort in the body but generally we can't place our finger on the exact problem. We have feelings of helplessness but can't explain why. We find it hard to function normally but again we don't know why. This chakra is also very sensitive to detecting adverse environmental stresses such as geopathic stress, bad ley lines and toxic pollutants.

**Higher crown chakra:** This is located above the head. This is our higher connection to spiritual enlightenment. When this is functioning correctly we feel at one with the world and all that exists in it. We understand and accept that we are all one and as such we are all a divine spark of pure light. That we are 'one' with the divine creator. Everything in our life brings us joy and we rejoice in this joyfulness. However, when this centre is not functioning correctly, we feel spaced out. We are very open to delusion and will follow pathways that are not ours. This will lead to discontentment with the spiritual life because we feel that it has lead us on a merry pathway that has not brought the happiness we sought.

**Spleen chakra:** This chakra is situated below the left armpit. It governs our assertiveness and empowerment. When it is functioning correctly we will be able to assert ourselves with confidence. We will feel a connection with our inner power and be comfortable to use it to help us move forward through life. However, imbalances will create anger issues, feelings of irritation with the body turning in to attack itself. If the centre is too open, people will be able to draw on your energy, leaving you depleted. This chakra is connected directly to our immune system. When others draw off our energy it will deplete our immune system, leaving us open to dis-ease.

**Past life chakra:** This is situated three fingers breadth behind the ears, just above the bony ridge. This is the centre of all our past lives. It carries all our memories and hereditary issues. When this centre is functioning correctly we 'know' our pathway forward. We have a connection with what we need to fulfil in this lifetime. We are self-directed and have the confidence to go with it. However, imbalances will hold you in the past. You will repeat past life patterns or ancestral patterns that have been passed down through the family.

If these past-life patterns are not broken, then people from the past can continue to have an effect on you. This is particularly true where we have experienced a difficult or abusive relationship. The person will retain their hold over you and control your actions even though they are no longer present in your life. The inbuilt patterns of the person will be deeply imprinted in this chakra and you will need to clear the blockage to be able to move on in life.

The chakras can be seen as the spiritual side of us while, below, the endocrine glands will be described so you can see how the chakras relate directly to the physical body and it's functioning. All chakras rotate in a clockwise fashion. They do so to draw in the universal energy that is present in the atmosphere and then it is sent down through the body to create health or life-force within us. Each chakra will rotate at a different speed. The base chakra will rotate at a slower speed than the crown chakra. This is because the colours associated with them have a frequency range and the chakras will rotate according to this. Red is lower down on the spectrum than violet and is therefore denser and will spin at a slower pace. When our chakras are rotating at their optimum frequency range we have perfect health. This is because they feed energy directly into the endocrine system which is the main control system for the body.

# Endocrine glands

These glands are the controllers of the body. They operate to keep the physical body working, whereas the chakras work to keep the energetic bodies working. The two are intricately connected and work in conjunction with one another. An imbalance in one will show up as an imbalance in the other.

## The Adrenal Glands

These are situated above the kidneys. They sit one on each kidney like a cap. Each gland has two distinct parts: the inner medulla and the outer covering, called the cortex. They both secrete hormones.

**The Medulla** secretes adrenalin and noradrenalin. These two hormones are known as the 'fight or flight' hormones. They prepare the body for the extra effort needed when faced with a dangerous situation, to cope in stressful situations or when needed to carry out a difficult task. The adrenal medulla is closely linked with the nervous system. When needed, the medulla will produce more adrenalin and noradrenalin, which makes the heart beat faster and more strongly, raising the blood pressure. The blood vessels near the surface of the body and in the gut will be constricted. This blood will be redirected towards the heart. This is one reason why we go 'white with fear'. Glycogen that is stored in the liver and muscles is turned into glucose, which will provide the extra energy needed for the 'fight or flight' reaction.

When the danger or stressful situation has passed, the

production of adrenalin and noradrenalin is reduced and the body returns to normal. However, if the danger or stress is constant, or if we are continually over-excited or under pressure, the body then remains in a state of 'preparation'. If this continues over a period of time it can lead to stress-related conditions such as high blood pressure.

**The Adrenal Cortex** is wrapped around the medulla. It secretes various hormones known as steroids, the most important of which are aldosterone and cortisone.

Aldosterone is one of the salt and water hormones. These hormones regulate water retention in the body. Aldosterone is a chemical messenger and tells the kidneys to reduce the amount of salt being lost in the urine. Salt determines the volume of blood being circulated, which in turn affects the heart's efficiency as a pump. Each molecule of salt is accompanied by a large number of water-molecules. This means, when we lose a lot of salt we will also lose a lot of water, which will affect the volume and pressure of the circulating blood. As a result, the heart will have difficulty in pumping enough blood around the body.

The secretion of aldosterone is controlled by the hormone renin which is produced by the kidneys. When aldosterone is low, the kidneys produce renin and the hormone level rises; when it is too high, the kidneys reduce their level of activity and the amount of hormone in the blood returns to normal.

Cortisone is one of the main sugar hormones. It is responsible for raising the level of glucose in the blood. Glucose provides the body with energy or fuel. In times of stress etc., cortisone is responsible for triggering the conversion of protein into glucose. There are many hormones involved in the maintenance of sugar levels in the body but cortisone is the most important.

As well as playing a key part in metabolism (the life-maintaining processes of the body), cortisone is also vital to the functioning of the immune system (the body's defence against illness and injury).

Cortisone, because of its crucial function in the body, is under strict control. The pituitary gland is responsible for this control. The pituitary secretes ACTH, which stimulates cortisone production. When the level of cortisone is too low, the pituitary secretes ACTH and the level rises; when it is too high, the gland slows the production and the level of cortisone falls.

The adrenal glands are associated with the base chakra. The base chakra nourishes and governs the kidneys and spinal column.

**The Gonads** are represented in the male by the testes and in the female by the ovaries. During puberty the gonads begin to grow and become active. This is influenced by the gonadotropic hormones, which are produced by the pituitary gland. These hormones stimulate the production of the sex hormones: testosterones in the male and oestrogens in the female.

These sex hormones stimulate the growth of the genitalia as well as secondary sexual characteristics such as the growth of body hair in both sexes, the growth of the larynx in the male (which produces the breaking of the voice), and the onset of menstruation, in the female. The testes in the male are responsible for the production of the sperm and the ovaries in the female are responsible for the production of the eggs.

The gonads are associated with the secondary or sacral chakra. The sacral chakra nourishes and governs the reproductive systems in male and female, our own sexuality and the emotional balance concerning that.

**The Pancreas** is one of the largest glands in the body. It is two glands in one. The most important hormone it secretes is insulin. It is also an exocrine gland, one that secretes into the gut (or another body cavity), rather than into the blood. It is situated across the upper part of the abdomen, in front of the spine. The duodenum is wrapped around the head of the pancreas. The pancreas has collections of secreting cells called acini. These are situated around the blind ends of small ducts. Each duct joins up with ducts from other acini until all of them eventually connect with the main duct running down the centre of the pancreas.

Among the acini are small groups of cells called the Islets of Langerhans. These are the cells that make up the endocrine part of the pancreas by secreting insulin, which is needed to control the sugar levels. The purpose of insulin is to keep the level of sugar in the blood at a normal level. A lack of insulin causes the condition diabetes.

If the level of sugar in the blood begins to rise above a certain amount, then the Islets of Langerhan respond by releasing insulin into the bloodstream. This acts to oppose the effects of hormones such as cortisone and adrenalin (which raise the level of sugar in the blood). Insulin allows sugar to pass from the bloodstream into the body's cells to be used as fuel.

The pancreas is associated with the third chakra or solar plexus. This chakra governs our relationship with ourselves. It is about our own personal power, our self-will.

**The Thymus** is found in the upper part of the chest, just behind the breast bone. The thymus is at its largest when we are young. After puberty it starts to shrink. The thymus assists the lymphatic system and it contains many of the lymphocytes, which are important in the body's defence against disease. Lymphocytes are found in the blood, the bone marrow, the lymph glands and the spleen.

The outer layer of the thymus is called the cortex. It contains many lymphocytes. The inner part of the thymus is called the medulla and also contains lymphocytes as well as other types of thymus cells. In early life the thymus is involved in programming the body's response when it has an infection. It also ensures that the body does not turn and attack its own tissues.

There are two main types of immune cells in the body and they are both types of lymphocytes. The thymus controls the T or thymus cell lymphocytes, which are responsible for the recognition of foreign substances and for the many ways in which the body attacks them. The other sort of immune cell is the B lymphocytes and these are responsible for manufacturing anti-bodies to foreign substances.

The thymus gland is associated with the fourth or heart chakra. This chakra governs our beliefs about love and relationships.

**The Thyroid/Parathyroid gland** is situated in the neck, just below the larynx. There are two lobes to the gland, and they lie just in front and at either side of the trachea as it passes down the front of the neck. The thyroid gland makes the hormone thyroxin. This hormone controls the body's metabolic rate (how effectively it converts food into energy). The thyroid gland contains iodine that is vital for its activity. The iodine is trapped in the gland and a lack of iodine in the diet can cause a condition called endemic goitre. The parathyroids are four tiny glands situated behind the thyroid gland. They play a major part in controlling the levels of calcium in the body. Calcium is a vital mineral because it is needed for the formation of bones and teeth; and it plays a role in the workings of the muscles and nerve cells.

The body's calcium levels have to be kept within certain boundaries, otherwise the muscles stop working and fits may occur. This is where the parathyroid glands come into play because they keep the calcium levels balanced. If the level of calcium is too low, the parathyroids produce parathyroid hormone in increasing amounts, which has the effect of releasing calcium from the bones to raise the level of calcium in the bloodstream. Conversely if the levels of calcium are too high, the parathyroids reduce or halt the production of parathyroid hormone, thus lowering the level of calcium in the bloodstream.

The thyroid/Parathyroid gland is associated with the fifth or throat chakra. This chakra governs all forms of communication. It is the link between how we communicate and our emotional expression of the heart centre.

**The Pituitary gland** is considered the master gland. Not only does it produce its own hormones but it also influences the hormonal production of the other glands. It is situated in the base of the brain, and is connected to the hypothalamus by a stalk of nervous tissue. The pituitary works closely with the hypothalamus to control many aspects of the body's metabolism (the various chemical processes that keep the body functioning). The pituitary gland is divided into two halves, the back half (posterior pituitary) and the front half (anterior pituitary).

The posterior, connected to the hypothalamus, concerns the production of two main hormones, both of which are actually produced by the hypothalamus. These two hormones are the antidiurectic hormone and oxytocin.

Antidiurectic hormone controls the water in the body. It acts on the kidneys affecting their ability to retain or release water.

When this hormone is released into the blood the kidneys tend to conserve water. When it is not secreted more water is lost from the body in the urine.

Oxytocin hormone is concerned with starting labour and causing the uterus to contract. It also plays a part in the starting the secretion of milk from the breasts. In males it is thought to play a role in generating an orgasm.

The anterior pituitary produces six hormones. Four of which control other glands in the body: the thyroid, the adrenals and the gonads. The anterior pituitary also produces two hormones follicle stimulating hormone and luteinizing hormone, which affect the sex glands. These hormones stimulate the production of the two major sex hormones, oestrogen and progesterone. The other hormone, that the anterior pituitary produces, is called the growth hormone. This hormone, as the name suggests, promotes normal growth.

The pituitary gland is associated with the sixth or third eye chakra. This chakra governs our intuition.

**The Pineal gland** controls the release of the hormone melatonin which has an effect upon the modulation of sleep patterns in both seasonal and circadian rhythms. It is shaped like a tiny pine cone and is located near the centre of the brain between the two hemispheres.

The pineal gland is associated with the seventh or crown chakra. This chakra governs our higher spiritual mind.

By now you should begin to see a very strong connection between the physical body and our spiritual body. The functioning of the physical body is controlled by the functioning of our spiritual body. The chakras work with the endocrine glands to control the functioning of the body at optimum health. The chakras control every aspect of the physical body, from our endocrine glands to our emotions and acceptance of our self! One system can't function without the other as they are interlinked on all levels. 'A spiritual soul living in an earthly body' is a term that many hear but don't truly understand. However, when we start to realise the interconnectedness between the physical body and spiritual body we can begin to see what they mean.

Perfect health is controlled by the perfect functioning, or spin, of the chakras to their frequency according to their colour. However, day to day challenges will affect this rotation. When we become stressed over money, for example, the base chakra will start to rotate faster. The adrenal glands will also respond by working harder to counteract the stress. This was how our bodies were designed. When the stress levels decrease the adrenals slow down and the base chakra will return to its normal frequency range. This is how it should be, but our lives today are far more stressed and few of us can actually return to a normal level of 'no stress'.

We tend to carry the stress of one thing onto another and the base chakra works faster and faster until it becomes blocked and stops spinning. Likewise, the adrenal glands continue to work harder and harder until they too become depleted and can no longer 'react' to the fight or flight response. The body then becomes tired and we feel out of sorts. If this continues for long enough other areas of the body associated with the base chakra will start to show dis-ease, such as kidney or bone problems. Anaemia is a classic example of a base chakra being out of sync or blocked, because the red blood cells are produced in the bone marrow.

We now understand that we are energy. This energy is controlled by the chakra system, which in turn controls the endocrine system. This much is clear, so how does ill-health actually manifest? Well, we can be likened to a door lock. The lock itself has several chambers for which a key is needed to open the lock. Each chamber in the lock needs to be turned for the lock to open, or each of the chambers needs to be opened to have health. The chambers represent our different aspects. Ill health is formed by an imbalance in the body where the chambers are set to closed. This is a slow process where each chamber of the lock is closed one by one over usually a long period of time. So how does ill health first start? That is simple ...we think it into reality!

# Our thoughts ...and their real importance!

'We are what we think' ...this is the most important thing to remember in life! This is because our thoughts are energy. When we think something we are in fact creating that thought-form into a state that stays with us. Our thoughts are what control's everything we feel and experience in and around us. This is probably the hardest thing for people to accept. Our thoughts are an energy that we are producing every single moment of the day. Hundreds of thousands of thoughts run through our brain daily. Some we are conscious of; others we are not.

So, if we are producing this energetic cloud of thoughts around us, what happens to it? Firstly, the energy will create either a positive cloud of energy, 'Happy thoughts', or a negative cloud of energy, 'Unhappy thoughts'. This will collect around the aura of the body and remain there.

Now, if we go back to our science days at school, you may remember that 'like energy' attracts 'like energy'. Positive attracts positive, negative attracts negative. So, if we have lots of positive energy surrounding us, we will attract more positive energy, which will make us feel even happier. We will feel that we are flowing through life on the right path. We will experience little stress because we will be 'at one' with the universe. We will know that for any challenges we face, a solution will present itself. Our chakras will pick up on this positive energy and will rotate at the correct frequency. We will also be attracted to other positive people, which will help us to remain more positive. Result = HEALTH.

However, if we are stressed and in a negative mood, complaining of everything going wrong in our life we will be creating a powerful cloud of negative energy. This will hang around our aura clogging it because negative energy is a denser energy than positive energy. It has a lower frequency. This cloud of negative energy will attract more negative energy because like attracts like. Hence we will feel more depressed and stressed than ever. We will also attract other negative people to us. The chakras will have to work faster to deal with the clogged aura and an imbalance will be created. Result = DIS-EASE = DISEASE.

This ebb and flow of energies happens all day every day. Most of the time we can clear the imbalance by returning our thoughts to a more positive perspective, balancing the chakras again. We need to be aware when the stresses of everyday life continue to affect us emotionally to the point where we cannot draw back to a more positive perspective. Traumatic events, relationship breakups, loss of work, loss of money can all have an enormous impact on the body and the emotions. They are challenges that can be difficult to come to terms with. They will have an impact on our chakras creating imbalances and blockages. If these persist they will start to create illness or dis-ease in the body. At first the symptoms will be small but the longer the imbalance persists the greater the illness will become. Such illnesses as cancer are created by just such imbalances that have been allowed to continue for years.

So the first chamber of the lock can be connected to our thought patterns. The second chamber is linked to the chakra system. Our thoughts create the negative energy, which starts to imbalance the chakra system. Once the chakra(s) are affected the third chamber of the lock, which is linked to the endocrine system, will be affected. Once this system is affected it will impact on the physical body. So the symptoms or the illness is the fourth chamber of the lock. The tangible illness that we see and feel!

In order to bring balance back to the body we need to align all the chambers of the lock. Aligning one or two will not bring lasting results. Holistic therapies work on the mind (chamber one), soul (chamber two), body (chamber three) and ultimately the whole person (chamber four). However allopathic medicine works on the illness (chamber four) only. The given medicine bypasses the other chambers and opens the last chamber. The first three chambers are forced open as the key is thrust into the lock and wiggled until a result is found, i.e. the medicine clears the symptoms. Sometimes, the first chamber is opened by the person's faith that the medicine will work. This is why some medicines and placebo pills work. Blind faith can open the chamber and, if this blind faith is strong enough, it can even open the second chamber. Such faith can bring the chakras back into alignment, as the negative thought pattern is removed and a positive outlook is seen. When the chakras are aligned, the third chamber is then also opened, as the chakra works directly with the endocrine system. In these cases, blind unwavering faith can bring healing results with the use of medicines but, in most cases, they only bring temporary relief.

Once the lock is forced open it remains open for a limited period of time before the body will try to close it again. Once the overriding negative thought patterns reach an optimal level the lock will close again and the medicine will no longer work. Usually another medicine is tried and this can set up a lifetime pattern of changing medications every few years. However, with a more holistic approach where all the chambers are opened one by one, the root cause of the problem is cured permanently.

The whole body is brought back into balance and true health will prevail.

There are many different ways we can help to bring our bodies back into balance holistically. The following section is a self-help section. It contains ideas for you to try. Some will work for you; others may not be so successful. Find those that do and change your life forever. This is your time to take your healing in your hands. It is your time to empower yourself. We all have the ability to heal ourselves. Use the chakra chart to find the chakras related to whatever dis-ease you have and work to bring those chakras back into balance.

If you are unsure which chakra you need to work on, then start with the base chakra and work up to the crown chakra. Or, if you feel guided, work with all chakras at the same time. Check your thoughts and make sure you are always thinking positively and not attracting negative energy! Go with what you feel is right. There is no right or wrong way. Trust in your gut instinct. This is the first step to taking back your power, so enjoy it. Do not be disappointed if the results are slow to show themselves. You may have taken years to create the imbalance so it will not be corrected in a few days but have the faith to know that each day you will be working towards a new, healthier you.

# Part 2 Self-help section...

# Crystals

Crystals have been used since before Atlantian times (a very long time ago!) to bring balance to the body. They work through resonance and vibration. They are formed in Mother Earth and have been placed here for us to use to bring balance to our chakras. They are a gentle but effective treatment. They treat the body holistically. That is to say, they work on the physical, emotional, mental and spiritual bodies. They realign the subtle energies and dissolve any blockages of energy, which cause dis-ease within the body. Crystals work at rebalancing the root cause of the dis-ease. This way, the dis-ease is cleared completely. They work by rebalancing the aura and chakras, clearing physical and psychological dis-ease.

Most dis-ease in the body is caused by a combination of factors. The imbalance may be emotional or mental, or a sign of spiritual disconnection. Energy imbalances can cause the chakras to rotate too fast, too slow or not at all. The imbalances, when very severe, can cause the aura to become detached from the body in places. This causes many problems as we are more susceptible to other people's negative energy. Normally, when our aura is strong, we can deflect others negative energy more easily, including any negative or naughty entities that are present. These are spirits who still walk the earthly plane because they either don't realise they are dead or are scared to pass to the light (heaven), because they were not 'nice' while they were alive. They generally mean us no harm but do have a detrimental effect on our energy levels. They can feed on our energy and we are left feeling exhausted at times and wondering why!

Environmental stresses such as electromagnetic smog from computers, TV's, microwaves etc. and geopathic stresses can also have more of an effect when our auras and chakras are out of sync. Sick-building syndrome is found to be more prevalent where people have imbalances in their energy systems.

Crystals can be used not only to rebalance the body but to show us why we have the illness. This is an important factor because we can learn from the mistakes that caused the dis-ease in the first place. They are also a great aid when the dis-ease has a past-life link. Many crystals can be used to help clear past-life traumas. They show us the underlying cause from our past life, so we can work to clear it from our present life.

# How to use crystals

Crystals can be worn as jewellery, carried in a pocket or laid on or around the body. Wearing as jewellery is one of the easiest ways of using crystals because you can wear them all day without having to consciously do anything with them. If they are worn as jewellery, provide an amethyst or quartz bed to lay the jewellery on at night, as this will clear any negative energy that they have absorbed during the day. Crystals can be placed on the body at the chakra centres. This will help to bring balance and clear any blockages from the chakras out to the aura.

## You can place them according to their colours:

Red crystals- base chakra. Place on the groin area or one crystal at the top of each leg.

Orange crystals- sacral chakra. Place on top of the belly button.

Yellow crystals- solar plexus. Place at the base of the sternum. This is where the rib cage meets in the middle of the chest.

Green or pink crystals- heart chakra. Place in the centre of the chest between the breasts.

Pale blue- throat chakra. Place in the indentation at the base of the throat.

Indigo blue - brow chakra. Place between the eyebrows.

Violet, white or purple crystals - crown chakra. Place next to the top of the head.

Otherwise, you can use them according to their healing properties. For example, a green crystal may be placed on the solar plexus to bring healing to this centre. Many crystals have multiple uses and can be used on different chakras. If you feel drawn to place a crystal on a chakra that isn't usually used on that chakra, then go with your intuition. I am always using crystals on chakras that they aren't usually used on, but it always has a good result!

Crystals can also be carried in a pocket during the day and placed next to your bed at night. Again they can be placed on an amethyst or quartz bed to be cleansed of the day's accumulation of negative energies.

Crystals contain an elemental deva inside them. These devas are the spirit protectors of the crystals. They are there to help us and like to be treated with respect, so always remember to thank the crystals for their healing energy. Crystals can become your best friend. Crystals are always there for us in times of need, they give us guidance, they rebalance our energy and they don't answer back! What more could you want in a best friend!!

Another way of using crystals is to meditate with them. One or more crystals can be used, again be guided by your intuition. This is your time to take back your power. Every time you make a conscious decision to heal yourself you are reinforcing your inner power. So trust in your gut instinct or just choose a crystal that attracts you. Hold the crystal/s in your hand or place them on or around you during your meditation. Again this is your healing; everyone will have a different way of using their crystals. There is no right or wrong way. Trust in yourself and enjoy the healing process.

# Choosing crystals

There is an abundance of crystals on the market to buy, which can make choosing the right one a bit daunting. There are many ways to choose. Looking through the crystals listed farther down can give you a good starting point. Choose a crystal that covers the imbalance/s that you are trying to heal. There may well be more than one, so compile a short list of those that interest you. Then go to a good crystal shop and look and hold each one of the crystals on your list. You will be drawn to some but not to others. Sometimes a crystal will shine brighter than the rest or it will create a tingling sensation when held. This is the crystal's way of getting your attention!

At some time, we might be gifted a crystal by someone. These are always special and should be treasured. If you are still unsure which crystal is right for you, your birth stone can be used as a guide. This will connect you to your zodiac sign and earth energies.

## Crystals and the Zodiac

**Capricorn Dec 22$^{nd}$ - Jan 19$^{th}$** Amber, Aragonite, Azurite, Carnelian, Fluorite, Galena, Garnet, Green & Black Tourmaline, Jet, Labradorite, Magnetite, Malachite, Onyx, Peridot, Quartz, Ruby, Smoky Quartz, Turquoise.

**Aquarius Jan 20$^{th}$ - Feb 18$^{th}$** Amethyst, Aquamarine, Amber, Angelite, Atacamite, Blue Celestite, Blue Obsidian, Boji Stone, Chrysoprase, Fluorite, Labradorite, Magnetite, Moonstone.

**Pisces Feb 19th - March 20th** Amethyst, Aquamarine, Beryl, Bloodstone, Blue Lace Agate, Calcite, Chrysoprase, Fluorite, Labradorite, Moonstone, Smithsonite, Sunstone, Turquoise.

**Aries March 21st - April 19th** Amethyst, Aquamarine, Aventurine, Bloodstone, Carnelian, Citrine, Diamond, Fire Agate, Garnet, Jadeite, Jasper, Kunzite, Magnetite, Orange Spinel, Pink Tourmaline, Ruby, Spinel, Topaz.

**Taurus April 20th - May 20th** Aquamarine, Azurite, Black Spinel, Boji Stone, Diamond, Emerald, Kyanite, Kunzite, Lapis Lazuli, Malachite, Rhodonite, Rose Quartz, Sapphire, Selenite, Tiger's Eye, Topaz, Tourmaline, Variscite.

**Gemini May 21st - June 20th** Agate, Apatite, Apophyllite, Aquamarine, Blue Spinel, Calcite, Chrysocolla, Chrysoprase, Citrine, Dendritic Agate, Green Obsidian, Green Tourmaline, Sapphire, Serpentine, Tourmalinated & Rutilated Quartz, Tiger's Eye, Topaz, Tourmaline, Ulexite, Variscite, Zoisite.

**Cancer June 21st - July 22nd** Amber, Beryl, Brown Spinel, Calcite, Carnelian, Chalcedony, Dendritic Agate, Emerald, Fire Agate, Moonstone, Moss Agate, Opal, Pearl, Pink Tourmaline, Rhodonite, Ruby.

**Leo July 23rd - Aug 22nd** Amber, Boji Stone, Carnelian, Cat's or Tiger's Eye, Chrysocolla, Citrine, Danburite, Emerald, Fire Agate, Garnet, Golden Beryl, Green & Pink Tourmaline, Kunzite, Larimar, Muscovite, Onyx, Orange Calcite, Petalite, Pyrolusite, Quartz, Red Obsidian, Rhodochrocite, Ruby, Topaz, Turquoise, Yellow Spinel.

**Virgo Aug 23rd - Sept 22nd** Amazonite, Amber, Blue Topaz, Carnelian, Chrysocolla, Citrine, Dioptase, Garnet, Magnetite, Moonstone, Moss Agate, Okenite, Opal, Peridot, Purple Obsidian, Rubellite, Rutilated Quartz, Sapphire, Sardonynx, Smithsonite, Sodalite, Sugilite.

**Libra Sept 23rd - Oct 22nd** Ametrine, Apophyllite, Aquamarine, Aventurine, Bloodstone, Chiastolite, Chrysolite, Emerald, Green Spinel, Green Tourmaline, Jade, Kunzite, Lapis Lazuli, Lepidolite, Mahogany Obsidian, Moonstone, Opal, Peridot, Prehnite, Sapphire, Sunstone, Topaz.

**Scorpio Oct 23rd - Nov 21st** Apache Tear, Aquamarine, Beryl, Boji Stone, Charoite, Dioptase, Emerald, Garnet, Green Tourmaline, Herkimer Diamond, Hiddenite, Kunzite, Malachite, Moonstone, Obsidian, Red Spinel, Rhodochrosite, Ruby, Topaz, Turquoise, Variscite.

**Sagittarius Nov 22nd - Dec 21st** Amethyst, Azurite, Blue Lace Agate, Chalcedony, Charoite, Dark Blue Spinel, Dioptase, Garnet, Gold Sheen Obsidian, Labradorite, Lapis Lazuli, Malachite, Okenite, Pink Tourmaline, Ruby, Smoky Quartz, Snowflake Obsidian, Sodalite, Spinel, Sugilite, Topaz, Turquoise, Wulfenite.

# Caring for your crystals

When you buy a crystal it will need to be cleansed before you start to use it. This is because it would have absorbed any negative energy around it. There are different methods to do this. All are effective so choose one that suits you best.

Crystals can be placed under running water to wash all the negativity away. As you hold them under the water hold the intention that the water is cleansing them. Then put out in the sun for a minimum of one hour to energize them again.

Immerse the crystals in a bowl of salt water. Holding the same intention as above and place in the sun for a minimum of one hour.

Make sure the crystal is not friable (water soluble) or you will slowly be dissolving it away! **Friable crystals**: Amber, Azurite, Calcite, Dioptase, Kyanite, Selenite, Sulphur, Zeolite.

Immerse the crystals in the sea, again holding the same intention to cleanse the negative energy away, but hold the crystals tightly as they have been known to 'jump' out of your hand never to be seen again! Place in the sun for a minimum of one hour.

Smudging with an incense stick. Hold the crystal in the smoke and hold the intention of the smoke cleansing the negative energy away. Place in the sun for a minimum of one hour.

Place on either a quartz or amethyst bed. This is a natural flat piece of crystal with lots of terminations to it. Leave the crystals overnight and they will be cleansed by the morning.

Place your crystal in a small bowl and cover completely with either salt or brown rice. Leave overnight for the energies to be absorbed into the rice or salt. Gently clear any remaining particles off the crystal and throw the rice or salt away.

Some crystals are self-cleaning such as Azeztulite, Citrine, and Kyanite. I would just rinse them to clear any dust or brush the dust off.

# Programming your crystal

Crystals can be programmed for specific purposes. If you have a long-standing illness that you want to heal, you can programme your crystal for that specific healing. Emotional hang-ups, mental conditioning, can also be helped by programming your crystal. The fact that you are 'verbalising' your wish to clear an area of your life that is giving you problems, is the first step to helping you heal yourself.

Sit quietly, holding your crystal in your hands. Feel its shape. Look at it from every angle. Notice any marks on it. Now look at the colour of it. Start to see it in all its beauty. As you do this you will start to form a connection with it. State that the crystal is dedicated for the highest good of all who use it. You do this by saying aloud and with meaning, "I dedicate this crystal for the highest good of all who use it or come within its sphere of healing energies". Now, when the connection feels right, ask your crystal to help you particularly with whatever you wish to heal.

A simple, "please crystal can you bring me back into balance so that I may experience complete joyful health", will suffice, or you can be more specific about voicing what help you need. The choice of wording is for you to decide. Just remember to be clear about what you need. Sit for a few moments sending the intention of your healing wishes into the crystal. Once you feel it has taken the intention, then bless and thank your crystal. Now it is ready to help heal you! Carry your crystal with you every day and know that its energies are working to bring balance back into your life.

Most of all enjoy each day as it presents itself to you.

# Crystal list

## Agate

This is a good grounding stone. If you feel that your head is in the clouds and you find it difficult to stay focused, then this will help to bring you back down to earth. It is a very calming stone, helping to protect and stabilise your energies. It brings balance to the emotional, physical and intellectual areas and can be used where a lot of emotional trauma is being experienced. Agate harmonises our yin and yang, the female and male energies. It soothes and calms us working slowly but, as it does so, it brings with it great strength and courage. It will bring to the surface any hidden information about why we are experiencing imbalance in our life. Agate aids self-confidence, self-analysis and acceptance of the self. It brings to one's attention any dis-ease preventing well-being– clearing emotional bitterness in the heart, emotional trauma and dissolving internal tensions.

It raises consciousness and encourages one to speak your truth. It also enhances creativity.

Agate stabilizes the aura, eliminating and transforming negative energies, making it a powerful cleanser of emotional and physical levels. Place it on the heart chakra to heal emotional dis-ease that prevents acceptance of love. Place on the abdomen to stimulate the digestive process and relieve gastritis. Agate is healing to the eyes, stomach and uterus. It cleanses the lymphatic system and the pancreas. It also strengthens the blood vessels and heals skin disorders. Agates come in different forms but they will all have the above properties as well as those listed below.

**Blue Lace Agate** – Blue lace agate is a gentle, calming stone that engenders tranquillity and brings peace of mind. It activates and heals the throat chakra and encourages you to speak truthfully. It can ease the 'harsh edge' off communication in difficult times, enhance public speaking, and smooth discussions. Blue lace agate is a healing and nurturing stone, dissolving old patterns of repression and allowing a new mode of expression. It is an inspiring stone that can assist inner attunement, and has been used to perform miracles. The calming energies can be used to cool anger. It assists in flight, grace, reaching higher Spiritual planes, and communicating with angels.

Physically, it has been used to aid arthritis, headaches, digestive issues and bones. It is a powerful throat-healer. By clearing blocked self-expression, it releases shoulder and neck tension. It is good for thyroid deficiency, throat and lymph infections. It lowers fevers and removes blockages of the nervous system. It also helps the capillaries and the pancreas.

**Moss Agate** – This is a stabilising stone strongly connected to nature. It refreshes the soul and helps you see the beauty around you. It will help to reduce any sensitivity to the weather and to pollutants. Otherwise known as the 'Midwives stone' it helps with the birthing process by lessening pain and ensuring a good delivery. Moss agate is a stone of new beginnings, it releases blockages – a stone of abundance and wealth, helping you to access your intuition as well as your more practical side. It improves self-esteem and will enhance more positive personality traits. A balancing stone that releases fear and deep seated stress, it helps one to get along with others more easily. It will inspire new ideas after a period of stagnation. It encourages self-expression and communication. Moss agate will give insights into why one is unhappy with life or depressed. It is an 'optimistic' stone.

Physically moss agate will speed up recovery after illness. It will cleanse the circulatory and elimination systems, and encourage the flow of lymph. It is anti-inflammatory and will boost the immune system. It helps depression, hypoglycaemia, dehydration, treats infections, colds and flu.

# Amazonite

This is one of the best crystals to calm and soothe emotional aggravation. Soothing to the nerves it dispels irritating and negative energy. Soothing to all of the chakras; especially the heart, thymus and throat chakra.

Amazonite enhances our communication concerning love. It balances our male and female energies bringing clarity and aligning the aura as it goes. It is a stone of good health, helping you to manifest and maintain universal love. It is thought to enhance intuition, psychic powers, creativity and intellect.

Good for the nervous system because it dissipates any energy blocks. It is high in calcium and aids calcium assimilation. Protects against tooth decay, osteoporosis and diminishes calcium deposits within the body. It also helps to dispel muscular spasms.

# Amber

This is one of the best tonic stones for the body. It allows the body to heal by absorbing negative energy and transmuting it into positive energy. It will draw dis-ease and negative energy out of the body and replace it with positive energy. Amber is also a very powerful chakra cleanser. It emits bright, soothing, sunny energy, to calm nerves and enliven the disposition, helping when you wish to manifest things into your life. Stimulating to the intellect, it opens the crown chakra. It enhances decisiveness and strengthens the memory. Amber aligns ethereal energies to the physical, mental and emotional bodies and balances the aura. It is therefore a good stone when you are stressed. It cleanses the environment where placed and is good to purify rooms for birthing and re-birthing. It purifies the body, mind and spirit. It treats goitres, throat problems, eyes, kidneys, bladder, liver, gall bladder, alleviates joint problems and strengthens the mucous membranes.

# Amethyst

This is the stone of sobriety. It is said to help heal alcoholism, compulsive behaviours and addictions of all kinds. It is a very spiritual stone with a high vibration. When worked with, or worn, it will raise your vibrations. Its serenity enhances higher states of consciousness and it is excellent for meditation. Amethyst balances the mental, emotional and spiritual bodies, clearing and stabilising the aura. It is a stone of protection and will protect against psychic attack. It will enhance stability, strength, calmness, invigoration, balance, courage, inner strength and peace. It can help you find your path in life. It is also reputed to be beneficial when dealing with legal problems, and money issues, which can lead to prosperity and abundance. Dispelling anger, rage, fear and anxiety, amethyst is a calming stone.

Physically it can help with arthritis, hearing disorders, strengthening the skeleton, nervous system, endocrine system, chronic fatigue, fibromyalgia, digestive tract, heart, stomach, skin and teeth.

# Apatite

Apatite connects one to a higher level of spiritual guidance and eliminates negativity in yourself and others. It is extremely useful in the expansion of knowledge. It increases your motivation and builds up your energy reserves. Apatite helps to raise Kundalini energy, inner clarity, and creates a sense of oneness with the higher-self and assists one in reaching deeper states of meditation. It helps us to be more open and socially at ease. It helps to harmonize, balance, and bring together the physical, intellectual, emotional, and spiritual bodies.

Apatite is useful in inspiring the development of clairvoyance, clairaudience, and clairsentience and can help you to access past-lives, which are having an impact on your current life. It balances the male and female (yin-yang) energies and stimulates your creativity and intellect. It clears confusion and helps access information to be used personally and for the collective good. Apatite helps to ease sorrow, anger and apathy and reduces irritability and overcomes exhaustion. It clears frustration and endorses passion without guilt. It is helpful for hyperactive and autistic children. It can heal bones and will encourage the formation of new cells. Aids absorption of calcium and helps cartilage, bones, teeth, motor skills, and hypertension. It is thought to ameliorate arthritis, joint problems and rickets. It will suppress hunger and raise the metabolic rate. Apatite is healing to the glands, meridians and organs. Use with other crystals to enhance their healing powers.

# Aquamarine

Aquamarine has the calming, soothing energy of the sea. This is the stone of courage that reduces stress, fears and quiets the mind. It is tranquilizing, uplifting, encouraging openness and innocence. It enhances creativity, communication, self-awareness, confidence and purpose. It invokes tolerance of others. Aquamarine encourages taking responsibility of the self and breaks old self-defeating patterns. It clarifies perception and clears up confusion and is good when feeling overwhelmed by one's life.

Aquamarine brings closure where needed, sharpens intuition and opens one up to clairvoyance. A good meditation stone that shields the aura and aligns the chakras. It clears the throat chakra, bringing communication from higher levels. It is good on the throat, spleen and heart Chakra. It is used for protection on journeys, especially those who travel on water. It has an effect on the etheric and mental levels. Aquamarine helps stabilize and harmonize unsettled surroundings and helps one attune to nature.

Recommended as a purifier of the throat it helps sore throats and swollen glands. It harmonises the pituitary and thyroid by regulating hormones. It is a tonic to the body and also helps eyes, jaw, teeth and stomach. It is detoxifying and calms an overactive immune system (helpful for autoimmune diseases and hay fever).

# Aragonite

Aragonite is an earth healer and grounding stone. It transforms geopathic stress and clears blocked ley lines. With its ability to centre and ground physical energies, it is useful in times of stress. It gently takes you back into childhood or beyond, to explore the past. Psychologically it teaches patience and acceptance, it combats over-sensitivity, encourages discipline and reliability and develops a pragmatic approach to life. Mentally, it aids concentration and brings flexibility and tolerance to the mind. Emotionally, it combats anger and emotional stress, providing strength and support. Physically, it is a stone that makes you feel comfortable and well, within your own body. Spiritually, it stabilises spiritual development, restores balance and prepares for meditation by raising your vibrations and bringing energy into the physical body.

Physically, it strengthens the immune system and regulates processes that are proceeding too fast. It helps Reynaud's disease and chills. It aids calcium absorption, heals bones, and restores elasticity to discs. It also ameliorates pain, and stops night-twitches and muscle spasms.

# Aventurine

Enhances our creativity, and imagination, as well as intellect and mental clarity. It is a stone of prosperity and brings career success. It brings a sense of calm and balance and enhances happiness. It helps one to see alternatives and potentials in all situations, giving a positive outlook, motivation, courage and inner strength. It is also said to bring luck, especially in games of chance. Aventurine brings friendship into one's life and enhances leadership and decisiveness. It is also a stone of protective energies and is good against vampirism of your energies (when someone draws energy from you without your consent or knowledge). It balances male and female energies, and mental, emotional, physical and auric bodies. It has a strong connection to the Devic realm and can be used to guard against geopathic stress.

It treats lungs, heart, adrenal glands, muscles and the urogenital system. It helps relieve stammers and severe neuroses bringing understanding of what lies behind the condition. It is beneficial for blood and the circulatory system, headaches, general health, and sleep disorders. Aventurine is associated with the heart chakra.

Aventurine comes in blue, green, red and peach. They all have the same abilities as above and blue and green have the following extra properties as well.

**Blue Aventurine** – Excellent mental healer.

**Green Aventurine** – Brings harmony and healing to the heart. It dissolves negative emotions and thoughts. An all-round healer that brings emotional calm and wellbeing. It settles nausea and is useful in malignant conditions.

# Azurite

Azurite brings clear understanding and expands the mind. It helps to release long-standing communication blocks. It helps you to let go of long-standing programmed belief-systems and aids you to move forward into the unknown without fear. Emotionally this is a good stone to clear stress and worry, grief and sadness, allowing in more 'light'. It transmutes fear and phobias and brings the understanding of why they occurred in the first place.

Azurite treats arthritis and joint problems, aligns the spine, clears throat problems, and works at a cellular level to restore any damage to the brain. It can be used to heal kidney, gallbladder and liver problems. Useful for the spleen, thyroid, bones, teeth and skin. A stone of detoxification of the body. Azurite has a special affinity with the mind and mental processes.

## Black Tourmaline

Black tourmaline, also known as Schorl, is associated with the root or base chakra, and is excellent for grounding excess energy. It is a purifying stone that deflects and transforms negative energy, and thus is very protective. It can transform and remove negativity from an individual or an environment. It is often used as an aura cleanser, and can help one attain higher levels of awareness. Black tourmaline is also used for repelling and protecting one from black magic, and is often said to return the negative spell to the sender. It diminishes fear by promoting understanding of the self and self-confidence.

Black tourmaline has also been used to deflect radiation energy from TV's and computer monitors. It helps maintain one's spirits even after receiving messages of doom and gloom. Emotionally, black tourmaline is excellent for dispelling fears, obsessions, and neuroses, bringing emotional stability.

Physically, black tourmaline can strengthen the immune system; help with heart disease, arthritis, dyslexia and gout. It balances and stimulates the adrenal glands.

## Bloodstone

Bloodstone is a healing stone for base, navel, solar plexus and the heart chakra. It is the stone associated with courage, abundance, purification and good fortune. It helps one to accept the turmoil associated with change. It helps overcome anxiety, depression and melancholy. Balancing the mental, emotional and physical bodies, it brings harmony, adaptability and strength. It renews relationships and helps your love life. Bloodstone helps with the decision-making processes and helps in attuning to the spiritual realms. It provides vitality, boosts talent, organizational abilities and charitable instincts.

Bloodstone can help to cure psychosomatic illness (one with more emotional roots than physical) and pains. It also purifies the blood and detoxifies the organs, especially liver, kidneys, bladder and spleen, by neutralising the toxins and eliminating them. It is helpful in cases of Leukaemia, failing eyesight, lung congestion and rashes.

# Calcite

Calcite is a powerful energy-cleanser and amplifier. It removes negative energy from the environment simply by being in a room. It removes stagnant energy from the body. It accelerates spiritual development and aids channelling, psychic abilities and astral travelling. It is a stone of motivation, combating laziness. Calcite calms the mind and teaches discernment. It boosts the memory and is good to use when studying. It is a good mental healer, dissolving rigid beliefs and old programmes and restoring balance. It alleviates emotional stress and replaces it with serenity. Calcite is a stabilising stone, which helps one to trust in one's own abilities. It aids willpower and the ability to overcome setbacks.

Calcite cleanses the organs of elimination, helps constipation, helps calcium uptake in bones, dissolves calcifications, strengthens the skeleton and joints, and stimulates blood clotting and tissue healing. It strengthens the immune system and comes in an array of colours each of which has the above properties as well as others associated with their colour.

**Black calcite** – Use this stone to go back to past lives. It can help in unlocking the past to deal with anything that is affecting the current life. It helps the soul to return to the body after trauma or stress. It helps to alleviate depression and is good when you are having fearful thoughts during the night.

**Blue calcite** – A gentle calming stone, helpful when recuperation is needed. It helps in communication issues, especially where there is dissent. Blue calcite can absorb energy, filter it and return it to the benefit of the sender. It gently soothes the nerves, lifts anxieties and releases any emotional stress. It lowers blood pressure and dissolves pain on all levels.

**Clear calcite** – This is a powerful detoxifier. It is a 'cure all' stone that clears and aligns all the chakras. It heals at a deep soul level.

**Gold calcite** – This is a great meditation stone. It helps one attain a connection with higher planes, making us more mentally alert. It is particularly good for the sacral and crown chakras.

**Green calcite** – A good mental healer, as it dissolves rigid beliefs and old programmes and then restores balance to the mind. It helps to clear away anything that no longer serves us. It is a powerful immune booster, which absorbs negative energy and clears the body of bacterial infections. It is helpful with arthritis, constrictions of the ligaments or muscles and with the realignment of bones. The green ray is cooling to fevers, burns and inflammations. It will soothe any anger-generated dis-ease.

**Orange calcite** – This is a great energising and cleansing stone, which can be used on any of the lower chakras. It helps to balance the emotions, clears fear, and overcomes depression. It is useful for the reproductive system, gallbladder, intestinal disorders (IBS) and helps to clear mucus from the body.

**Pink calcite (Mangano calcite)** – This has connections with the angelic realms and is a good heart stone. It helps us to forgive, release fear and grief from the heart centre. It brings unconditional love, aiding our self-worth and self-acceptance. It helps to prevent nightmares. It is good to use when one has suffered a trauma of any kind. Healing to nervous conditions, it lifts tension and anxiety.

**Red calcite** – A base chakra stone that is both energising and healing. It increases one's energy, uplifts the emotions, aids willpower and opens the heart chakra. It clears fear and helps one to understand its origin. It clears blocked energy that is preventing your stepping forward in life. It clears constipation, heals hip and lower limb problems, and loosens the joints.

**Yellow calcite** – An uplifting stone that is good at eliminating that which is holding us down. It stimulates the will. It is good for relaxation and meditation. It stimulates the higher mind. Use on the crown and solar plexus chakras.

# Carnelian

An inspirational stone of creativity, individuality and courage. It is a member of the agate family and, as such, has protective energies. Protecting against envy, jealousy, fear and rage. It stimulates analytical precision and awakens one's inherent talents, stimulating inquisitiveness and initiative. It is good at dispelling apathy, indolence and passivity. It can aid memory, including recall of past lives. It can assist one in finding the right mate. In addition, it can help with manifestation of one's desires, and brings good luck. Carnelian can help ease or remove sorrows from the emotional body. It increases personal power, energy and compassion. It also helps stabilize energies in the home. It is sometimes called the 'actors' stone'. Carnelian is associated with the root and sacral chakras.

Carnelian has been used to heal open sores, colds, pollen allergies, rheumatism, kidney stones and other kidney problems, gall stones and neuralgia. It rejuvenates tissues and cells and is useful in aiding disorders of the spine, spleen and pancreas.

# Celestite

This is the stone of balance, alignment and deep peace. It heals the aura and reveals the truth. It teaches us to trust the infinite wisdom of the divine. Its calming energies cool fiery emotions. It sharpens the mind, disperses worry and promotes mental clarity. It aids fluent communication.

This healing stone dissolves pain and brings in an abundance of love. It can be used to treat the eyes and ears, to eliminate toxins and to soothe tense muscles. It is good for any throat problems.

# Chalcedony

This is a nurturing and optimistic stone promoting brotherhood. It enhances group stability so is good when groups of people are working together. Chalcedony helps thought transmission and enhances telepathy. It is good for absorbing and dissipating negative energy, so is good for placing in a room where you spend a lot of time. It brings the mind, body, emotions and spirit into harmony and balance. It removes hostility and transforms melancholy into joy. Chalcedony eases self-doubt and aids constructive inward reflection. Opening the mind to new ideas and helping acceptance of these new ideas and situations. It imparts mental flexibility and verbal dexterity, so is useful when learning new languages. It also improves the memory.

Chalcedony is a powerful cleanser for open sores. It fosters one's maternal instinct and increases lactation. It improves mineral assimilation and combats mineral build-up in the veins. It is thought to lessen the effects of dementia and senility. It increases one's energy levels, heals the eyes, gallbladder, bones, spleen and blood and aids circulation. It aids the regeneration of mucus membranes and helps disorders caused by weather sensitivity (glaucoma). It boosts the immune system, stimulates lymph and banishes oedema. It has an anti-inflammatory effect, lowers temperature and blood pressure. It heals the lungs from the effects of smoking.

# Charoite

This is a stone of transformation. It stimulates our inner vision and enhances spiritual development. It connects the heart and crown chakras and links us to the higher levels. Charoite facilitates the acceptance of others. It releases fear and puts everything into proper perspective. Showing us how things really are. It is a good stone for releasing worry and dissolving stress, bringing with it a sense of relaxation. It can help one overcome compulsions and obsessions. Mentally, charoite is a stimulating stone and, physically, an energising stone. It is good at transmuting negativity.

Charoite is good for helping with problems of exhaustion, blood pressure, eyes, heart, reversing liver damage due to alcohol, cramps, aches, and pains. It helps insomnia and can help enhance our dreams. It is good for cases of autism and for bi-polar disorders.

# Chrysoprase

This is a very balancing and energising stone and will bring the male and female (yin/yang) energies into balance. It aligns the chakras, especially the heart chakra and brings in universal energy to the physical body. It helps with co-dependency. Chrysoprase is a good stone for deep meditation. It gives one personal insights into the self to help self-love. Chyroprase dissolves the ego and shows us any self-defeating patterns. It also heals the inner child. It is a stone of forgiveness and compassion, opposing judgementalism. It encourages fidelity in both business and personal affairs. It is also good for stimulating speech and enhancing one's mental dexterity.

Chyrsoprase helps with the assimilation of vitamin C. It is also useful for the heart, liver, reproductive organs, detoxifying, clearing nightmares, claustrophobia, removing heavy metals from the cells, gout, eye problems, balancing hormones and fungal infections.

# Citrine

Citrine is known as the 'wealth' stone because it is said to promote success and abundance, especially in business and commerce. Citrine is purported to bring good fortune, sometimes in very unexpected ways. It enhances mental clarity, confidence, self-esteem, motivation, happiness and will-power. Citrine is a good protective stone and is a powerful cleanser of the chakras, clearing and aligning the aura with the physical body. It is warming, energising and creative in its energies and is one of the few crystals that doesn't need to be cleansed, because it doesn't hold onto negativity. It is a stone of joy.

It is said to alleviate depression and self-doubt and diminish irrational mood swings due to its effect on mental clarity. It improves and encourages self-expression, and helps overcome difficulty in verbalising thoughts and feelings. It brings about an inner calm so one's own wisdom can be found. It releases negative traits, fears and feelings. It also releases the past, fear of responsibility and can help stop anger. It is associated with the solar plexus chakra.

Citrine is said to aid digestion and helps eliminate nightmares that disturb one's sleep. It also balances the emotions, helps CFS (chronic fatigue syndrome), depression, phobias, spleen, reverses degenerative diseases, pancreas, clears kidney and bladder infections, blood and circulation, thyroid gland, constipation, cellulite, and the eyes.

# Diamond

Diamond is an energy amplifier. It increases the energy of anything with which it comes into contact, so is especially useful when used with other crystals. It is a stone of abundance and wealth. Excellent at clearing electromagnetic stress and protecting against phone radiation. Diamonds cut through emotional and mental pain, reducing fear and helping new beginnings. It re-energises the aura.

Diamonds treat allergies and glaucoma, aid the brain and sight and can also be used to rebalance the metabolism.

**<u>Herkimer diamonds</u>** – They clear electromagnetic pollution and radioactivity and can block geopathic stress. They energise, enliven and promote creativity. They clear and open the chakras so that we can connect to our higher selves.

They protect against radioactivity and treat all disease caused by it. They correct DNA, cellular disorders and balance the metabolism, clearing tension and stress from the body.

# Emerald

This is a stone of inspiration and infinite patience. It is often referred to as the stone of 'successful love', bringing domestic bliss and loyalty. It enhances unconditional love and keeps a partnership in balance. If it changes colour it is thought to signal unfaithfulness. It is a good heart stone and opens the heart chakra bringing emotional calm. Helping one to enjoy life to the full, it helps to overcome any of life's setbacks and gives the energy to recover and start again. It enhances memory and mental clarity. It is a stone of wisdom.

Physically, emerald treats sinuses, heart, lungs, spine, muscle's and is soothing to the eyes. It detoxifies the liver, alleviates diabetes and rheumatism. It is said to improve the vision.

# Fluorite

Fluorite is a stabilising stone promoting spiritual and psychic wholeness. It produces order within the mental, emotional, physical and spiritual bodies. It brings order where there seems to be only chaos. It aids impartiality and detached reasoning where needed and is a stone of discernment and aptitude. It protects psychically and in the physical realm. It helps one meditate and learn to go past the 'chatter' that our minds tend to generate when first learning to meditate. It helps with one's concentration and to develop orderly, sequential thoughts, removing mental blocks. Fluorite can help build relationship skills. It is a good aura-cleanser.

Fluorite comes in different colours, each one having extra properties to the above. Clear fluorite guards against psychic attack and strengthens consciousness.

Physically it helps general health throughout the body's main skeletal and muscular systems. It purifies, cleanses and eliminates any disorder in the body. It helps the teeth. At the start of the illness, it dissipates disorders such as tumours, colds, flu, Staph and strep infections, infectious cankers, herpes, and ulcers. It treats the structure, composition and cell formation of bones and helps with DNA and RNA damage to the cells of the body.

**Blue fluorite** – protects emotions and restores emotional balance.

**Purple fluorite** – strengthens mystical insight, psychic awareness, and can open the third eye.

**Green fluorite** – is an all-purpose healing stone that promotes healing on all levels. It also promotes self-love.

# Garnet (red)

Garnet is a powerful cleanser and re-energiser for the chakras. It revitalises, purifies and balances energy, bringing serenity or passion as appropriate. Inspiring love and devotion, it is a stone of commitment. It fortifies, activates and strengthens survival instincts, bringing courage and hope to seemingly 'hopeless' situations. It turns crisis to challenge.

Garnet balances the sex drive and alleviates emotional disharmony. It stimulates past-life recall and sharpens perceptions of oneself and others removing inhibitions and taboos. It opens the heart and bestows self-confidence. Garnet activates other crystals and amplifies them. It dissolves ingrained behaviour patterns that no longer serve. It revitalises feelings and enhances sexuality, bringing warmth, devotion, understanding, trust, sincerity and honesty to a relationship. It helps control anger, especially toward the self. Red Garnet is good for the Root Chakra and the Heart Chakra.

Garnet regenerates the body and stimulates the metabolism. It treats disorders of the spine and spinal fluid, bone, cellular structure and composition. Purifying to the heart, lungs and blood, and regenerates DNA. It aids assimilation of minerals (iodine, calcium, magnesium) and vitamins (A, D, E). Garnet boosts the immune system and energy levels.

## Hematite

Hematite is a stone for the mind; it helps in sorting things out. It helps with attunement, memory, original thinking and technical knowledge. Hematite is good for mathematical pursuits. It develops mental and manual dexterity, encouraging you to reach for the stars and helping you with dissolving self-limiting concepts. It balances the yin and yang, and stabilises the physical and etheric bodies. It is balancing for the mind, body and spirit and dissolving negativity. It attracts kind love. A grounding stone, bringing clarity and tranquillity into one's life. It is good for self-control and inner happiness. Hematite is good for the base chakra.

Hematite helps leg cramps, blood disorders, nervous disorders, insomnia, and heals breaks and fractures. Place a piece of hematite at top of spine and at base of the spine to realign the vertebrae.

# Howlite

This is an extremely calming stone. It links to the higher spiritual dimensions, opening attunement and preparing the mind to receive insights and wisdom. It assists with out-of-body journeying and helps one to access past lives. Place on the third-eye to access other lives. It helps to formulate our ambitions and helps us to achieve them. A good stone to teach oneself patience. Howlite helps to eliminate anger and uncontrolled rage. Keep a piece in your pocket and it will absorb your own anger and any that is being directed at you. It helps one to overcome criticalness and selfishness, strengthening positive character traits. It stills the mind.

Howlite physically, balances calcium levels within the body and aids teeth, bones and soft tissue. It eliminates pain, stress and rage.

## Jasper

This is the nurturer stone. It supports us during times of stress and brings tranquillity. Shows us we are here to assist others not just ourselves. A stone of protection and grounding to the physical body. It aligns the aura and the chakras, cleansing them and absorbing any negative energy. It balances the yin and yang, and aligns the mental, emotional and physical bodies with the etheric bodies. It clears environmental and electromagnetic pollution. Jasper imparts determination and gives one the courage to pursue problems assertively. Stimulating the imagination, it transforms ideas into action. Jasper is a supportive stone after prolonged illness and helps to re-energise the body.

Jasper comes in a variety of colours and types. Each contains the same basic properties plus extras as listed.

**Brown Jasper and Picture Jasper** – These are connected to the earth energies and are therefore very stabilising and balancing. They are good at taking you to deeper levels and helping one connect to past lives and revealing karmic causes affecting one's life now. Physically, they boost the immune system and detoxify the body. Brown jasper strengthens one's resolve to give up smoking.

**Dalmatian Jasper** – This is a stone of fun and is good when you are feeling depleted of energy. Dalmatian jasper reminds us that we are spiritual beings on a human journey. It helps us to accept this joyfully. It contains tourmaline that quickly transmutes negative energy and outworn patterns that no longer serve us. It encourages a determination to succeed and to see ideas through, into action, which makes it a useful stone for those starting up their own business. It helps over-intellectual people or excessive thinkers to get out of their head and into their body. It helps move you forward in life. Emotionally, it encourages fidelity and harmonizes one's emotions. Helping to overcome potential revenge scenarios, dalmatian jasper is very grounding, imparting calm and tranquillity. It is beneficial for cartilages, nerves, reflexes and sprains. It guards against nightmares, night terrors and assists safe sleep.

**Flamingo Jasper** – This is a motivational stone with an 'Adrenalin kick'. It is very energising, especially after illness. It rectifies unjust situations by showing us the bigger picture. Its energies repel stalkers and ex's who won't let go. It is good for aiding dream recall. Physically, flamingo jasper calms an excessive libido. It balances the mineral content in the body and regulates the supply of iron, sulphur, zinc and manganese within the body. It supports the circulatory system, digestive and sexual organs, ameliorates allergies, and clears the liver and the bile ducts.

**Green Jasper** – This jasper balances out the parts of your life that have become all-important to the detriment of others. It heals obsessions. A good heart chakra stone.

Physically, it helps skin disorders, ailments of the upper torso, the digestive tract and dispels bloating. It also reduces toxicity and inflammations.

**Red Jasper and Brecciated Jasper** – These are gently stimulating. They are excellent worry beads to calm the emotions. They bring problems to light before they get too big, and provide the insights into how to solve them. They are good base chakra stones.

Physically, they strengthen and detoxify the circulatory system, the blood and the liver.

**Mookaite Jasper** – A stabilising stone to bring balance to one's inner and outer experiences. It encourages one to follow new experiences and instils a deep calm to face them. Mookaite encourages one to be more flexible in life. It shows us all the possibilities and helps us to choose the correct one.

Physically, it helps the immune system, heals wounds and purifies the blood.

# Kyanite

This self-cleaning crystal encourages one to speak the truth and cuts through fears and blockages. It opens the throat chakra to encourage self-expression and communication. Kyanite cuts through confusion, blockages, illusion, anger, and stress and stimulates the higher mind. It draws energy into the organs and aura.

It can be used to treat the adrenal glands, brain, fevers, muscular disorders, urogenital system, thyroid and parathyroid glands. It is good for pain relief, lowering blood pressure and healing infections.

# Labradorite

Labradorite is a magical transformational stone, it's an esoteric stone of knowledge. It is one of the best grounding stones to accompany astral travel and higher chakra work. It helps to maintain one's connection to Earth, whilst its light-reflectivity helps to explore higher vibrations. It ensures that you are able to bring down and integrate, into physical life, whatever you learn working in the higher realms. In meditation focusing on labradorite can help you enter and maintain the meditative state. Labradorite deflects unwanted energies from the aura and prevents energy leakage. It forms a barrier to negative energies shed during therapy sessions. It stimulates the intuition and psychic gifts. Strengthening one's faith in oneself and trust in the universe, it gets to the root of problems and calms an overactive mind. It energises the imagination, bringing up new ideas. It clears mental confusion and indecision and allows one to have self-understanding on a deeper level.

Labradorite helps the immune system. It treats disorders of the eyes and brain. It relieves stress and regulates metabolism and is good for treating colds, gout and rheumatism. It balances hormones, relieves menstrual tension, and lowers blood pressure.

## Lapis Lazuli

Lapis Lazuli is a powerful thought amplifier. Stimulating higher awareness, it brings clarity and objectivity. It opens the third eye and connects one with the consciousness of the Universe. It connects you to your spirit guides. Lapis lazuli is good at protecting you against psychic attack, and returning it to the source. It helps you to confront the truth and to accept its learning, harmonising conflict and aiding self-expression. Lapis Lazuli helps one with dream recall and psychic work. It harmonises the physical, emotional, mental and spiritual bodies. It clears depression and lack of purpose, dissolving martyrdom, cruelty and suffering. Lapis Lazuli will help towards successful relationships. Lapis is also a protective stone; given to children it helps to keep them out of danger. Lapis is very balancing for the throat chakra and the third eye chakra.

Physically, lapis lazuli helps with pain, migraines, headaches, respiratory problems, nervous system, throat, larynx and thyroid. It cleanses organs (especially the kidneys), bone marrow, thymus and the immune system. It is good for purifying the blood, reducing high blood pressure and assisting hearing. Lapis Lazuli effects female hormonal balance. It usually increases the menstrual cycle by two days, and for those that are menopausal, a sequence of changes is induced that may result in the return of a regular menstrual cycle. It aids weight loss by reducing the fat levels in one's tissues.

## Lepidolite

Lepidolite is a stone with extremely high vibrations. It is a stone of transition, releasing and re-organising old patterns, and then helping to induce change. It is good at clearing negativity. One can access the Akashic (past life) records using lepidolite and tune into past lives to clear blockages in one's present life. Lepidolite activates and opens the throat, heart, third eye and crown chakras, clearing blockages and bringing cosmic awareness. Good for reducing stress and depression, it is helpful in halting obsessive thoughts and despondency. It also stimulates the intellect and helps focus on what is important. It encourages one to reach goals and helps one to become more independent. Stimulating to the intellect it speeds up decision-making. It is a calming and soothing stone.

Lepidolite locates the site of dis-ease. It vibrates gently when placed on an area of disease and helps to clear the blocks. It relieves allergies, strengthens the immune system, restructures DNA and enhances generation of negative ions. It also relieves exhaustion, epilepsy and Alzheimer's. Lepidolite numbs sciatica and neuralgia and overcomes joint problems. It is a good detoxifier for the skin and connective tissue and is helpful during menopause. It treats illnesses caused by sick-building syndrome and computer-stress, and clears electromagnetic pollution.

# Malachite

A stone of transformation, it assists and supports you in changing situations. It is a powerful stone that will amplify both positive and negative energies, so should be used carefully. It will clear and activate all the chakras, especially the throat and heart, and help you connect to higher spiritual guidance. It is also toxic and should only be used in its polished form. Helping to clarify emotions, it will easily absorb any negative energy from the body and atmosphere and needs to be cleansed regularly on a quartz bed.

It also absorbs all kinds of radiation. Malachite will show what is blocking our spiritual path and has a strong affinity with the Devic kingdom. Place it on the third eye to activate psychic vision, and on the heart to bring balance and harmony. It will open the heart to unconditional love. When used on the solar plexus it will give deep emotional healing.

Malachite draws out deep-seated emotions and clears anything that is outdated and no longer serving us. It helps us to take responsibility for our actions. It goes to the root of the problem and shows us insights to help us move on. It helps us to absorb and process information better, especially difficult concepts. It helps us to 'see' the cause of disease, will alleviate shyness and aid friendships.

Physically, malachite will show us the cause of dis-ease. It is also helpful for cramps of all kinds and sexual dis-eases. It lowers blood pressure. Asthma, arthritis, epilepsy, fractures, joint problems, growths, vertigo, tumours, the pancreas and the spleen are helped by malachite. It aligns cellular structure and DNA and will boost the immune system.

## Moonstone

This stone is strongly connected to the moons energies and, like the moon, it shows us that everything in life is part of a cycle. Moonstone is a stone of new beginnings. It is a very good emotional calmer and healer. It enhances psychic abilities and clairvoyance. It will make conscious the unconscious and help to promote empathy. Its gentle female energies will calm an overly aggressive female or an excessively macho man. Emotionally, moonstone will soothe stress and stabilise emotions.

When placed on the solar plexus it will draw out and dissolve any outworn patterns that no longer serve us, bringing with it an understanding and emotional intelligence. Moonstone clears deep, emotional stress and will heal disorders of the upper digestive tract that are caused by this stress. Moonstone helps us to be more spontaneous, and allows the forces of serendipity and synchronicity to flow.

Physically it helps the female reproductive organs, PMS, menstruation and balances the hormones. It helps the digestive system, assimilation of nutrients, elimination of toxins, clears fluid retention, alleviates degenerative conditions of the skin, hair, eyes and helps fleshy organs (liver, pancreas). It is an excellent stone for conception, childbirth, and pregnancy.

## Obsidian

This stone is without boundaries or limitations. It gets straight to the truth of things and fast! It exposes one's flaws, weaknesses and blockages, and shows one the way to clear any that are destructive, that don't empower us for our highest good. It pushes us forward in life and lends us support as we go. Black Obsidian can be ruthless, so take care if you wish to use it. A gentler form is mahogany obsidian, snowflake obsidian or apache tear, but, if you wish to work with black obsidian then use in conjunction with rose quartz, which will surround you with the love needed to deal with any unpleasant issues that are brought up.

Obsidian can take you back to past lives to clear any festering emotions or trauma that need to be cleared. Obsidian is a very protective stone that absorbs negativity from the environment. It will block psychic attack and remove any negative spiritual influences. A large piece of obsidian can be used to clear geopathic stress and absorb environmental pollution, but don't place in an area where people may be affected by its truth enhancing properties. Obsidian brings clarity where needed and will clear any confusions or constricting beliefs. It is a stone that will bring you face to face with your shadow-side and will help you to integrate it and accept who you are.

Physically, obsidian shows us the root cause of dis-ease. It helps us to 'digest' anything that is hard to take and will help with the digestive tract. It's a good detoxifier. It helps with reducing arthritic pain, joint problems, cramps and injuries.

There are different types of obsidian each of which will contain the properties above as well as others as listed below.

**Apache Tear** – This is a form of black obsidian but is much gentler in its effect. It will bring up negativity but will do so slowly so it can be transmuted gently. Apache tear is excellent for absorbing negative energy and protecting the aura. It is a good stone for grief, showing one what the source of the distress is, and it helps one to forgive. It removes any self-limiting beliefs and will increase spontaneity.

Physically it enhances assimilation of vitamin C and D. It calms muscular spasms and is a good detoxifier.

**Black Obsidian** – This is one of the stronger obsidians that will go straight to the root of your problems and show your faults. Everything will be brought up for releasing. It helps to release that which no longer serves us so we may move on into the future with confidence. Black obsidian repels negativity and disperses unloving thoughts. It clears old loves and provides support during the changes. Use briefly on the third eye to break through mental barriers and dissolve mental conditioning. It draws together scattered information and promotes emotional release. Always use with rose quartz to help soften the blow of what's being brought up!

**Mahogany Obsidian** – This is gentler than the black obsidian and is connected to the earth energies, making it a good grounding and protective stone. It gives one strength in times of need. It eliminates energy blockages, vitalises purpose and stimulates growth on all levels. It provides deep soul healing. Its stabilising energy strengthens a weak aura and will align the sacral and solar plexus chakras. Place by the bed to clear mental stress and tension.

Physically it relieves pain and improves circulation.

**Snowflake Obsidian** – When used on the sacral chakra it will calm and soothe, while gently showing ingrained patterns of behaviour that no longer serve us. It balances the mind, body and spirit. It helps us to learn from our mistakes and to accept our successes.

Physically it is good for the skeleton and it improves the blood circulation and veins.

# Onyx

This is the stone of change. It imparts confidence for us to make changes and feel at ease in our surroundings. It connects us to a higher guidance, and can take us forward to view our future. Onyx is supportive in confusing or difficult times, and/or during times of enormous mental or physical stress. It provides us with the vigour, stamina and steadfastness that we need in such times. It helps you keep your own counsel. It is useful in past-life work for healing old injuries or physical traumas that are affecting one now. It will take you to the source of injury. Onyx heals old grief and sorrows. It is a mental tonic alleviating overwhelming fears and worries, balances our yin and yang, and will integrate any dualities within the self.

Onyx treats teeth problems, bones, bone marrow, blood disorders and the feet. It is best used on the left side of body.

# Petrified Wood

This is an excellent grounding stone. It will provide one with strength in all areas of one's life. It can be used effectively to access past lives when used in meditation. During illness it will provide the support and insight needed to heal. During the crisis period of an illness it shows you why you are suffering and the lesson that you need to learn from it, so the illness doesn't have to be repeated. It is a stone of transformation, helping you to reach higher levels of consciousness. A stone of patience, of slow, steady growth towards ascension. It helps you overcome limiting emotional patterns.

Physically, it treats atrophied portions of the body. It also helps with paralysis. It will strengthen the back and align the skeleton. Good for treating hearing loss and incontinence and, for balancing the liver and gallbladder. It is a good blood and liver cleanser, and aids proper blood-cell manufacture in the bone marrow.

# Prehnite

A stone of unconditional love. A stone to heal the healer. This has a strong affinity with the elemental realm and, when meditated upon, it can connect you to the universal energy grid, Archangel Raphael and your spirit guides. It aids precognition and develops trust in our inner knowing. It shows you your path forward in life. It has the ability to seal the auric field in a protective shield. Prehnite can aid dream recall. Use in gridding for peace and protection in the house and in the garden to create a haven of healing. Prehnite is a Feng shui stone for de-cluttering, it helps you to let go of possessions that you no longer need. Helpful for those who hoard possessions or love, due to inner lack. It alleviates nightmares, phobias and deep fears, uncovering and healing the dis-ease that created them.

Physically, prehnite is good for hyperactive children. It diagnoses dis-ease and clears the root cause. It is useful for the bladder, kidney, thymus gland, shoulders, chest and lungs. It treats gout and blood disorders and repairs the connective tissue in the body. It stabilises malignancy.

## Quartz

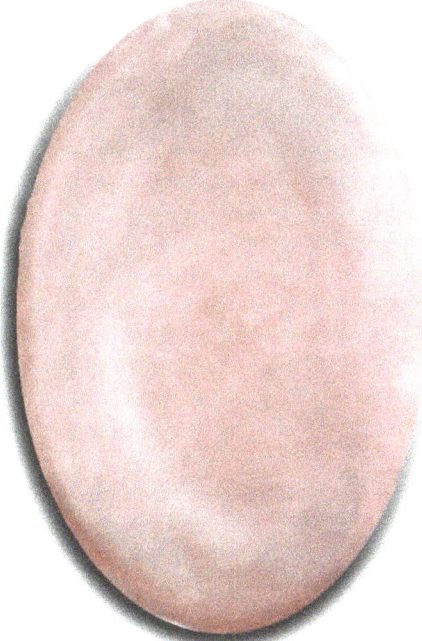

This is one of the most powerful healing and energy amplifiers. It absorbs, stores, releases and regulates energy, and is excellent for unblocking it. Quartz will work to the frequency of person being healed. It takes the energy back to before the illness set in. It will then cleanse and enhance the organs and subtle bodies so the body can heal itself. It is a deep soul cleanser, working on all levels. Quartz will enhance psychic abilities. Use in meditation to filter out distractions. It helps concentration and will unlock memory.

Physically, it treats the spleen, endocrine system and blood and stabilises the metabolic processes. Quartz is a 'Master' healer. It protects against radiation and dispels static electricity.

There are different types of quartz as well as the clear quartz covered above. Other quartz will have the above properties plus qualities as listed below.

**Blue Quartz** – Blue quartz, also called Dumortierite. It is a stone of order that can enhance organizational abilities, self-discipline, and orderliness. This is due to the effect it can have of balancing the throat chakra and enhancing communication between lower chakras (physical) and higher chakras (mental/spiritual). Blue quartz brings order to all things, releasing fears and bringing courage to one's life. It also boosts creativity and expression. Emotionally, it reduces problems of a scattered mind and disorganization, and brings mental clarity.

It helps one to see and accept reality. It helps one build new relationships. It can lift depression and replace it with peace and happiness. It helps clear stubbornness, particularly where it is ultimately bad for you. Blue quartz reduces emotional tension, enhances spiritual development, and aids contact with spirit guides and angels. It can also help to express your spiritual thoughts and dreams. Blue quartz is excellent for meditation. It generates electromagnetism, dispels static electricity and protects against radiation.

Blue quartz can help with cooling the body where overstimulation is present. It treats the throat, thyroid and parathyroid, detoxification, hyperactivity and blood. It is a master healer and helps stabilise the metabolic processes. Darker shades of Blue that are nearer to indigo, in colour, can also be used for the Third Eye Chakra.

**Rose Quartz** – The stone of unconditional love and infinite peace. This is the best heart crystal; it teaches us what 'true love' is. It is great to use in times of trauma or stress because its energies are very calming and reassuring. It will open and cleanse the heart chakra at a deep level so that you can learn to love yourself and others. Placed by your bed, rose quartz will bring a loving relationship to you if are looking for it. It is a good stone if you think yourself unworthy of love. This stone encourages self-forgiveness and acceptance. It helps to invoke self-trust and self-worth.

Physically it strengthens the heart and circulatory system. It helps lung and chest problems, heals the kidneys and will help alleviate vertigo. It soothes burns and is good for the complexion. Helpful in cases of Alzheimer's, Parkinson's and senile dementia.

**Rutilated Quartz** – This is fantastic at filtering negative energy away from the body. It also protects against psychic attack. This crystal gets to the root of problems and helps the transition to a new direction in life. It soothes dark moods and acts as an antidepressant. It relieves fears, phobias and anxiety, releasing constrictions and counteracting self-hatred.

It absorbs mercury poisoning from the blood, intestinal tract, muscles and nerves. Its vitality is excellent for energy depletion and exhaustion, and it is excellent for chronic illnesses. It treats bronchitis and the respiratory tract. Stimulating and balancing on the thyroid. Good for repelling parasites.

**Smoky Quartz** – This is a powerful base chakra stone, grounding us. It is a good anti-stress stone and will fortify one's resolve while experiencing difficult situations. It absorbs negative energies and replaces them with positive ones. It is good against geopathic stress and electromagnetic smog. Smoky quartz lifts depression and clears fears, even when they border on suicidal tendencies. It brings with it an emotional calmness and helps us to leave behind anything that no longer serves us. It helps clear the mind, aiding concentration and communication skills.

Physically it is a pain reliever and is good against headaches and cramps. It also treats problems of the abdomen, hips and legs, reproductive system, muscles, nerve tissue and the heart. It aids the assimilation of minerals and regulates fluids in the body.

# Rhodochrosite

A stone of selfless love and balance on all levels. It imparts a dynamic and positive attitude. Rhodochrosite is an excellent relationship stone, especially for people who feel unloved or who have suffered sexual abuse. It teaches the heart to assimilate painful feelings without shutting down and removes denial. A good stone to clear the solar plexus and base chakra of suppressed emotions and feelings. It will show you the truth about yourself and others, and help identify any underlying patterns. These can then be faced and cleared without excuses but with a loving awareness. It will improve self-worth and is an emotional calmer. An aversion to the stone means that you could be suppressing something that you don't want to face. This stone, mentally enlivening, encourages a positive attitude, enhances the dream state and helps creativity. Rhodochrosite is a stone of passion, encouraging the spontaneous expression of feelings.

Rhodochrosite is an irritant filter relieving asthma and respiratory problems. It is good for the circulatory system and purifies the blood and kidneys. It restores poor eyesight, normalises blood pressure, stabilises the heart beat and invigorates the sexual organs.

# Rhodonite

An emotional balancer, this stone encourages nurturing love. It makes an excellent first-aid stone for emotional shock and panic. Rhodonite reveals both sides of an issue. It will stimulate, clear and activate both the heart and heart chakra. It grounds the energy and is a yin and yang balancer helping you to achieve your highest potential. Good for abuse, emotional self-destruction and co-dependency, it clears emotional wounds and scars from the past, bringing up the emotions to be transmuted. Good in past-life clearing, in cases of abandonment and betrayal. Good in cases where we throw the blame at others for things we are unhappy about in ourselves, because rhodonite promotes unselfish self-love and forgiveness. It shows you that revenge is self-destructive. Rhodonite builds confidence and will clear confusion.

Physically, it is a wound healer, soothes insect bites and reduces scarring. It beneficially affects bone growth, hearing organs (fine-tuning auditory vibrations) and stimulates fertility. It treats emphysema, inflammation of joints, arthritis, autoimmune disease, stomach ulcers and multiple sclerosis.

# Ruby

This is a heart stone that encourages you to follow your bliss! It stimulates the pineal gland and promotes positive dreams. Mentally, ruby enhances awareness and concentration, and brings up anything negative for transmutation. A very protective stone, great where psychic attack or energy vampirism is a problem. This is a stone of potency and vigour easily overcoming exhaustion and lethargy.

It is a good detoxifier for the blood and lymph. Ruby treats fevers, infectious disease, impaired blood flow and assists the circulatory system and heart. Stimulating on the adrenals, kidneys, spleen and the reproductive organs.

# Sodalite

Sodalite unites our logical with our intuitive side. It opens our spiritual side and assists the import of information from the higher mind to the physical level. It is good for meditation because of its ability to stimulate the pineal gland and the third eye. Being a stone of truth, it helps you stand up for your beliefs. Sodalite will bring harmony and solidarity to groups. It stimulates trust and companionship and will eliminate mental confusion, encouraging rational thought, objectivity, truth and intuition. It calms the mind and clears old mind-sets and rigid thinking, allowing space for new to enter.

It is an emotional balancer. Helps self-esteem, self-acceptance and self-trust, and brings up our shadow qualities to be faced without judgement, so they can be accepted. Sodalite will clear electromagnetic pollution. Placed by a computer it clears any harmful emanations. It also helps sick-building syndrome and the associated dis-eases.

Physically, it balances the metabolism, overcomes calcium deficiencies, cleanses the lymphatic system and organs. It boosts the immune system, helps radiation damage, insomnia, throat, larynx, digestion, cools fever and lowers blood pressure.

## Sugilite

This is a loving stone, good for dissolving hostility, especially in groups of people. It encourages loving communications. Sugilite helps us to face up to unpleasant matters and gives us the loving support to see them through. It alleviates fear, grief, sorrow, and promotes self-forgiveness. It encourages positive thoughts and reorganises our thought patterns in a more organised manner. It shows any underlying learning difficulties, such as in dyslexia, and helps us to accept and overcome them. It releases emotional turmoil and can dispel despair. It draws off negative energy and replaces it with loving, healing energy. An excellent pain reliever it is good for headaches and discomfort on all levels. Treats epilepsy, insomnia, nightmares and nerves.

## Sunstone

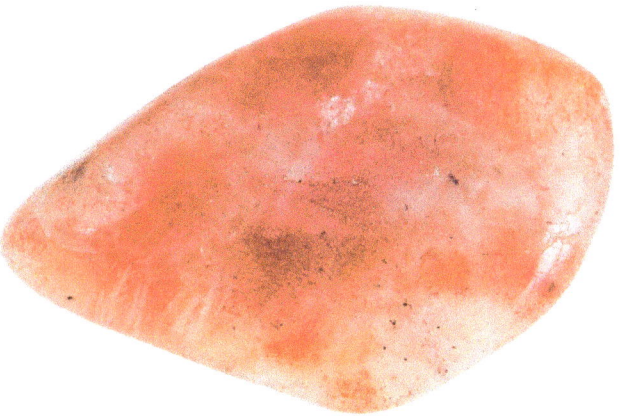

This stone of joy will restore the sweetness to life. It will clear and draw light into all chakras. This alchemical stone is connected to the sun energies and, when used during meditation or in everyday life, will draw these energies in for the benefit of the user. It heightens intuition. From both the chakras and aura, Sunstone removes energy-draining hooks, connecting to us from other people, lovingly returning them to the sender. It is good for cord-cutting after relationships have run their course. Sunstone removes co-dependency, helps self-empowerment, independence and restores one's vitality.

It is a natural antidepressant and will lift a dark mood. Good against feelings of discrimination and abandonment, sunstone removes feelings of failure, inhibitions and hang-ups. It encourages optimism and enthusiasm for life. Place on the solar plexus to lift out heavy or repressed emotions.

It is good for people who are pessimistic about life and great for SAD (Seasonal Affective Disorder). It stimulates self-healing powers, regulates the autonomic nervous system and harmonises organs. Chronic sore throat, stomach ulcers and depression can also be helped with sunstone. Gird around body to help cartilage problems, rheumatism, and general aches and pains.

# Tiger's Eye

This stone works with both the earth and sun energies. It is a good grounding stone when you are feeling spaced out or uncommitted. Good for psychic development and attunement of the third eye in 'earthy' people. It's a stone of practicality and insight and it anchors necessary change in the body. Good for resolving internal conflict of pride or wilfulness. It will balance the left and right spheres of the brain and is good when dealing with scattered information, because it will help bring it into a coherent whole. It eliminates the 'blues' bringing brightness and optimism into one's life. Tiger's eye will bring an awareness of both personal needs and those of others. Stimulating to the kundalini energy, it is thought to attract wealth.

Helpful for the eyes, night vision, throat, reproductive organs, broken bones, and asthma.

There are variations of tiger's eye. They have the same properties as tiger's eye with added properties as listed below.

**Blue Tiger's Eye** – Also known as Hawks Eye. It helps to enhance your psychic abilities. It brings to light awareness of personal needs and those of others. It enhances integrity of communication and practical communication. It can help you find courage to recognize thoughts and ideas, and the willpower to carry them into the physical realm. When stressed, it is good, as it has a calming energy. It aids overanxious, quick-tempered and phobic people. Blue tiger's eye can be used especially, to protect the upper chakras. It is also said to bring good luck and wealth to one who wears or carries it. Blue tiger's eye is associated primarily with the throat chakra.

Physically, it helps with the eyes, night vision, throat, reproductive organs, broken bones and asthma. It slows down the metabolism, cools an over-active sex drive and dissolves sexual frustrations.

## Tigers Iron

This promotes vitality throughout the whole body. A stone of change that takes you to a place of refuge when danger threatens. It is good for emotional and or mental burnout or family stress, giving us the strength to carry on. Very good when you are completely exhausted, it will help you find the space for contemplation and provide you with the energy to see things through. It stimulates creativity and will bring out inherent talents. Physically, it helps the blood, balancing the white/red cell count, eliminating toxins. It heals hips, lower limbs and feet, strengthening the muscles. It also aids the assimilation of vitamin B and produces natural steroids. Keep in contact with the skin for the best results.

# Topaz

Its vibrant energy brings abundance, joy and health. It brings our goals in life to fruition. This joyful stone imparts confidence, promotes openness and honesty and helps us to develop our inner wisdom. It stabilises the emotions and makes one receptive to love from every source. Mentally, topaz helps problem-solving.

This stone of health can help combat anorexia, aid our digestion, fortify the nerves, stimulate the metabolism and restore our sense of taste.

It comes in different colours but they all have the above properties as well as extra ones listed below.

**<u>Blue topaz</u>** – Particularly useful for the throat and third eye chakras and aiding in verbalisation.

**<u>Clear topaz</u>** – Purifying on the emotions and good at clearing trapped energy.

**Golden topaz** – Like a battery charger, this energises the body, strengthening our faith and optimism.

It strengthens the solar plexus and regenerates the cellular structure. Good for nervous exhaustion, it can be used to treat the liver, gallbladder and endocrine glands.

**Pink topaz** – A stone of hope. It eases out old patterns of dis-ease, dissolves any resistance and opens the way to vibrant health.

# Unakite

A stone of vision that balances the emotions with the spiritual. Use on the third eye to aid psychic vision. A good grounding stone to use in meditation. Several tumbled stones will bring calm energy to the environment, negating electromagnetic pollution from TV's if placed near. Good for re-birthing, bringing light to blockages so they can be integrated and released. Also good for past-life work, to find the source of a problem and be able to reframe it. Place on the third eye to do this. Unakite draws dis-ease from past and present to the surface, to be transformed.

A stone of convalescence, it is also helpful for the reproductive system, stimulating weight-gain where required, aiding a healthy pregnancy. It encourages the growth of skin tissue and hair. It balances the acid/alkali balance in body, stabilises the temperature in the body and helps with impotence.

This short list is of the more popular crystals to help you. There are many more on the market! If you feel drawn to any not on this list, then trust your gut instinct and go with it. You may find yourself drawn to one crystal but, after working with it for a while, may be drawn to choose another. In this case it is usually because the crystal has helped to discharge what was no longer serving you and it is time to release the next pattern. Take this as a positive sign and choose another crystal to work with. Some crystals will remain with you for many years while others will only remain a daily friend for a short time.

 I remember having a lovely quartz point that was my friend for many years. When my now ex-husband, decided that I should no longer have contact with anything esoteric he demanded that I throw all my crystals away. At the time, I was trying to shore up our marriage so I agreed …well almost! My quartz point was carefully wrapped and hidden in the depths of my jewellery box. It remained there for a few years until we moved from Germany to Spain. When unpacking and sorting my jewellery box I found it. He was at work at the time so I buried it next to a cactus that was in a large glass vase. You could only see the point if you looked very closely, and I knew he wouldn't as he had no interest in anything green and living!

 It remained in situ until the moment I decided on a divorce. It then came out and was put into daily use as my best friend. It helped me a lot through the tough times that followed. I managed to drop it several times, to my horror, but each time it remained undamaged, which is amazing considering that our floors in Spain are tiled. One day, however, when it flew out of my hand, it chipped up one side. It was like a staircase to look at and revealed the most beautiful rainbow. I knew that this chip was significant so I meditated with it.

 The message came to me that it signified how my journey was faring. I was heading towards the rainbow one step at a time. This brought me a huge amount of relief during a period in my life when I seemed to be at the very bottom of a deep pit with my 'ex' throwing everything at me. A few months later my crystal once again flew out of my hand… This time it was not my doing. It literally seemed to fly of its own accord. This time, however, it shattered into hundreds of pieces. I was heartbroken and just sat on the floor in floods of tears.

Luckily the kids were asleep so they didn't hear my despair. I collected all the pieces and wrapped them together, unsure what to do. I needed to discover why this had happened, so again I meditated. The message was simple…it was time for the crystal to go 'home'. It had served its purpose and I had to set it free, so I buried it lovingly in the soil where it would not be disturbed and gave thanks for all its help and support.

It was the first crystal that I'd had to bid goodbye, but it wasn't the last. Crystals will come into your life and will also leave it. Just remember, when they do, that you have reached another level and no longer need them.

Enjoy your crystals and all the love, learning, insights and friendship that they bring to you.

# Angels, spirit guides and ascended masters

## Angels

Angels are spiritual beings. They have no gender; they are neither male nor female. Certain angels are usually depicted as a male or a female but this tends to represent their energies rather than their sex. I tend to refer to Archangel Michael as a male and Archangel Ariel as a female for example, but that is because, for me, their appearance reflects the energies they represent. Angels are beings of light, which vibrate at a high level making it hard for most people to see them.

More people are becoming aware of their presence and are working with them to improve their lives. We all have a guardian angel, some have more than one. I have three who I use whenever I have a problem. Some people think they can only use angels if they follow a particular religion or are churchgoers. This is not true. Anyone can ask their angel/s for help. Some people see their angel using their third (spiritual) eye; some literally see them with their eyes, while others just sense them or find their calling card, which is a white feather.

Many dismiss these as dropping from a bird when, in fact, it is their angel trying to tell them that everything is okay. I have a little angel ornament sitting on a shell, which contains all my feathers. They bring me comfort and remind me that my angels are always around me. You can ask your angel to give you a feather but keep your eyes peeled as they can turn up in the most unexpected places. They can be large or small. Sometimes you may just see one drift past you while walking or driving. I have been known to chase a feather down the road to the astonishment of passers-by, or turn my kayak around to try to reach one that is floating on the sea. The angels like to have a little fun with us and these are a couple of their little tricks to put a smile on my face. Life at times can be difficult and challenging, so the angels like to try to lighten things up for us.

When we are born, many believe that we have a guardian angel to help us through our life. They are there as our guides and protectors. They sit patiently by, while we stumble through life, and will only step in, unasked, if we are in danger and it is not our time to pass over to the other side (die). Otherwise they can only assist us if we ask them to. That is because this is a planet of free will. That means that all the decisions we make are our own and we bear the consequences of those decisions.

If, because we have free will to choose, we make a wrong choice, our angels are not allowed to interfere even if they know it is not the right pathway and will not bring us what we seek in life. If, however, we ask for their help, they can give it and guide us onto the correct pathway. They will always support us even when we take the wrong pathway and will sit patiently hoping for an invitation to guide us! I suspect a lot of guardian angels sit by, heads in hands, imploring us to ask for help!!

There are many other than guardian angels. In fact, for every problem we have there will be an angel to help us. My most-used angel would be the parking angel!! I always call on one to help find me a space. There are also angels who help with car problems, computer problems, directions, getting an appointment...the list is endless but, if asked, one will help. By 'asking' I mean literally ask! You can speak aloud or ask quietly in your head. Either way works – they always hear us. Having asked, sit back and wait. If we don't appear to get what we want, it is usually because we humans, are incredibly impatient and don't like to wait!! When asking, don't demand what you want, or tell them how to make it come about– they don't like this any more than we would! When you do get what you asked for, then remember to thank them. Everyone likes to be acknowledged for the help they have given.

There are also the angels that are the next level up, so to speak. These are the Archangels. These are the angels that help us with our personal problems. Below is a list of the specific angels to help you enhance your life and make the changes that you need and want in your life.

## Archangel List

**Archangel Ariel** – Ariel means "Lioness of God". She is often depicted with lions, so if you keep seeing pictures of lions after enlisting her help you know she is near you. Call upon this archangel if you need to draw in the bravery or courage of a lion! She always gives us confidence in times of need. She can also be called upon when we need some divine miracles and magic to happen in our life. If you need to "manifest" something in your life that is connected to your life purpose, then call upon Ariel to help. Ariel's colour is pale pink.
Associated crystal: Rose quartz represents Ariel's loving energies. Keep one close to draw in Ariel's energies.

**Archangel Azrael** – His name means 'Whom God helps'. He is the angel who helps the helpers in life. Counsellors who help with grieving or dying people can call upon this archangel to back up their work and he will gently drop the right words of help into our ears. He is the archangel that surrounds people who are dying, and those who are left grieving, with his pale-yellow, loving light. He brings love and comfort in our time of need. If you wish to train as a counsellor, he can direct you to the best courses that will suit you. Very pale yellow is the colour associated with Azrael. You may see twinkly sparkles of this light when he is around.

Associated crystal: Yellow calcite is connected to Azrael's energies and holding or wearing yellow calcite can call in his energies to bring comfort when needed. You can even gift someone a yellow calcite and ask Azrael to surround the person with his love to help them through the loss of a loved one.

**Archangel Chamuel** – Chamuel means 'He who sees God'. He can be called upon when we need help to locate things, situations and people. He is especially good at helping us make the right career choice. He will ensure that our choice will match our talents and passions. When we have a career that is also our passion then our enjoyment in life increases and we know we are on the right path in life. Chamuel's colour is pale green like the new shoots that appear on trees in the springtime.

Associated crystal: Green fluorite will connect you to Chamuel's energies. Carry one with you especially, when going for interviews for work!

**Archangel Gabriel** – the name means 'God is my strength'. Gabriel is considered the next in line from God (the creator or the Divine light). Gabriel can help you tap fearlessly into the power of the Creator, reassuring us that it is ok to be powerful and also helping with written ability, especially if you work in an associated profession (journalist, author, screen writer, poet etc.). Gabriel is also associated with helping expectant mothers, through conception to parenting, and helping children. If you need some more 'play' time in your life to help you relax and de-stress then just ask, accept, and go where you are guided. Gabriel is associated with the colour copper.

Associated crystal: Citrine, or the metal copper. Keep either near you to connect to these helpful energies.

**Archangel Haniel** – Haniel's name means 'Glory of God'. Haniel can help you to live up to your highest potential in life, drawing out your hidden talents and polishing up your natural skills, so Divine magic can occur. This archangel's nurturing, mothering energy will surround you when you call for assistance, so she can bring miracles into your life. She can help us integrate all aspects within us including the dark or shadow aspects of ourselves so that we can see the beauty of our whole. Haniel's colour is bluish-white.

Associated crystal: Wearing or working with moonstones can draw Haniel close. She works with the cycles in life (moon, circadian rhythm) and can help us work with them, to clarify what we need in our life.

**Archangel Jeremiel** – Jeremiel's name means 'Mercy of God'. He is the archangel of mercy and can help us be merciful in our life towards both self and others. This is the archangel of life reviews. He can help us take stock and review what we have done in our life and guide us to amend the areas that are not working. He will show us what we have learned, where we have travelled from and to, and what old outdated patterns are ready to be released. He can also help us to be grateful for where we have reached in life. Jeremiel's colour is deep purple. If you see purple sparkles it is a sign that this archangel is near.

Associated crystal: Amethyst. Having one near will bring in Jeremiel's loving energies.

**Archangel Jophiel** – Jophiel's name means 'Beauty of God'. This archangel is connected with nature and our appreciation of the outside world. If you need to clear lower energies, spending time in nature and calling on Jophiel can help. Ask, and she will help us to find the time to chill out in nature and to appreciate it. When we are stressed we miss the beauty in the everyday. Jophiel can help you to appreciate what you have, showing you the beauty of the world around you.

Jophiel can be called upon to help when you need to spring clean your house, giving you a burst of energy and motivation. She can also help with redecorating, inspiring you on colours and decor. Deep rose-pink is Jophiel's colour.

Associated crystal: Pink rubilite will bring in Jophiels energies, so keep one near you.

**Archangel Metatron** – Metatron is the archangel of children and parents. If you need help with any child-related issues, then call upon Metatron to help guide you. He can provide what you need to help children: money, ideas, support, reassurance, time etc. He can also help with developing good organisational skills and can help you prioritise your life to what needs to be done first, to ensure that your life flows smoothly. Metatron was first a mortal man, living such a spiritually-rich life that he ascended into archangel-dom. Metatron's colour is violet with pale-green stripes.

Associated crystal: Watermelon tourmaline is the crystal of Metatron and carrying or holding one will draw his energies closer to you.

**Archangel Michael** – the name Michael means 'One who is like God'. He is thought to be the nearest to God (the Creator or the Divine light). He emanates the qualities of love, power, strength, motivation and unwavering faith. He is known as the protector angel and can be called upon to clear away any lower energies of fear we have or such energies associated with where we live and/or work. Archangel Michael is associated with the colour royal blue. If you feel that you need protection from any unpleasant energies or people, then you can surround yourself with the royal blue cloak of archangel Michael. Imagine putting a cloak over your shoulders and putting the hood up over your head. Then imagine zipping this cloak up from the floor all the way up to the top of your head. Once this is done you will be protected from any negative energies that are being directed at you. I used this protection for the three years it took to get my divorce. It made me feel more secure, knowing that Archangel Michael was around me. I used the cloak every morning before getting up. It was part of my daily ritual. I still use it when I sense any negative energy around me or if I just feel in need of a bit of extra protection.

Associated crystal: Sugilite will connect you to Michael's energies.

**Archangel Raguel** – Raguel means 'Friend of God'. He oversees all the other angels to ensure there is order amongst them. He is the angel of fairness and justice and will ensure that we act in fair and just ways. You can call upon him to shore up your faith in the goodness of humanity especially when it is tested. He creates harmony and order in relationships. If you find yourself in a dispute, then call him in to help guide you so that all parties involved are happy with the outcome. Raguel's associated colour is pale blue.

Associated crystal: Wearing or holding an aquamarine will connect you to Raguel's energies.

**Archangel Raphael** – Raphael means 'Shining one who heals'. He is the third in line from God (the creator or the Divine light). Raphael is the angel associated with healing. Raphael's colour is emerald green. You can ask him to surround you with his emerald-green light if you need healing in the body. He is also good at 'dropping' ideas into our heads. Just ask him for guidance about how you can improve your health and then be aware of any thoughts that just pop up. They might also come in the form of dreams or your being guided in a supermarket to the more healthy food section!

Raphael is also associated with safe travel and can be called in to protect us while we are in transit.

Associated crystal: Emerald or malachite will connect you to Raphael's energies so keep one near.

**Archangel Raziel** – His name means 'Secrets of God'. Raziel is the wizard of the archangel realm. He can help you with spiritual awakening and understanding. He has a way of expanding minds and how we think, enabling us to understand things that defy logic. He works with us in our dream state. When we go to bed we can ask him to help us with our spiritual awakening. In our dream state he will whisk our souls off to spiritual school, where we will learn things that will help us to advance our souls. You may not be aware of what has happened in the dream state but the knowledge is embedded ready for use when you need it. This archangel can also help us turn our ideas into reality as he is a master alchemist …he can help us, literally, to turn our ideas into gold! Raziel's colour is like a rainbow.

Associated crystal: Clear quartz will help connect you to Raziel's energy, especially clear quartz, which has a rainbow present in it. Look at the crystal and you may find a hidden rainbow in its depths.

**Archangel Sandalphon** – Sandalphon is the archangel of gentleness. Call upon Sandalphon to bring kindness to your words and actions. He is the archangel who is in charge of answering our prayers. All our prayers are heard. The answers might not come in the form we expect but they will be fashioned for our greatest good. All prayers are answered but we need to keep our eyes open to see the results. Sometimes we find it hard to receive from others so we can call upon Sandalphon to help us overcome our reluctance. This archangel loves music so when we play or listen to music we can call him in for help. Sandalphon was a mortal man who lived such a spiritual life that he ascended into archangel-dom. If you want to live a life of spiritual integrity, then call upon him to help you. Sandalphon's colour is turquoise.

Associated crystal: Cooling turquoise is the crystal connected to Sandalphons energy. Meditating upon this crystal can bring feelings of peace and calm into your life.

**Archangel Uriel** – Uriel means 'Fire or light of God'. Uriel is good at helping with intellectual pursuits and can help us with ideas, problem solving, answers and insights when we are stuck and don't know how to proceed. The 'answers' will pop into your head. If you need guidance on which direction will take you forward in life, he will illuminate the way, one step at a time. All you need to do is walk the path that 'feels' right. At each turn on the pathway you can ask him again for guidance to be sure that you are going the right way. Uriel is associated with pale yellow.

Associated crystal: Amber will connect you to Uriel's energy. Wear the crystal or just hold one while meditating and open your mind for the answers you are seeking.

**Archangel Zadkiel** – His name means 'Righteousness of God'. He can help to release emotional toxins from our heart. He is the archangel of forgiveness, of self and others. The best time to call on him is when we are about to go to sleep. Ask him to clear away any emotional baggage that no longer serves us. Request him to clear away, like a vacuum cleaner, all the emotional baggage that may be holding you back in life; or sit quietly, imagine a large dustbin in front of you and start throwing your unwanted emotions into the bin. Visualise the rubbish going in…words, stones, letters or anything that feels right for you. When the bin is full, or you feel you have no more to put in, ask him to turn it into divine love. This will transmute the negative energy into a positive energy. Thank him for his help and know that a clearing has occurred.

You might need to repeat this several times to clear everything out. Repeat the exercise as many times as feels right for you. You can specify what you want cleared or give him free reign to clear what he needs to clear. I prefer to let the angels clear what they feel is necessary as they have a bigger picture of what our life entails and look at it from an unbiased viewpoint. If we specify, we might miss parts that need to go, of which we are unaware. Zadkiel's colour is deep indigo blue.

Associated crystal: Lapis lazuli is the crystal connected to Zadkiel. Hold this crystal to the third eye to help open the ear chakras so you can 'hear' your divine guidance. Hold one during emotional clearing to help instil feelings of peace.

# List of the archangels, their associated crystals and what areas they cover.

| Archangel | Colour Association | Crystal Association | Helps With... |
|---|---|---|---|
| **Ariel** | Pale pink | Rose quartz | Bravery, confidence, courage. Divine miracles and manifestations. |
| **Azreal** | Very pale yellow | Yellow calcite | Counselling work/careers. Grieving and terminal illnesses. |
| **Chamuel** | Pale green | Green fluorite | Locating things, people and places. Helps with your career choice to match your inherent skills. |
| **Gabriel** | Copper | Citrine and the metal copper | Enhancing one's personal power. Aids our written ability. Helps us find time to play and helps expectant mothers to cope. |
| **Haniel** | Blueish white | Moonstone | Shows us our highest potential and draws out our hidden talents and skills so we can use them and integrate them into ourselves. |
| **Jeremiel** | Deep purple | Amethyst | Reviews Life and helps us to release old out-dated patterns which no longer serve us. |

| | | | |
|---|---|---|---|
| **Jophiel** | Deep pink | Pink rubelite | Shows us the beauty in nature. Clears us of lower energies. Can help with spring cleaning and redecorating the house! |
| **Metatron** | Violet and pale green stripes | Watermelon tourmaline | Helps with parenting and child-related issues. Shows us our priorities in life and helps us with our organisational skills. |
| **Michael** | Royal blue | Sugilite | Protects us from negative energies and helps with motivation and keeping the faith. |
| **Raguel** | Pale blue | Aquamarine | Shows us how to be fair and just when disputes arise. Helps to enhance harmony in relationships. |
| **Raphael** | Emerald green | Malachite, emerald | Healing, health issues, and leads us to a healthier lifestyle. Call upon him for safe travel. |
| **Raziel** | Rainbow | Clear quartz | He helps with our spiritual awakening and the understanding of it. He's a master in alchemy and manifestation. |
| **Sandalphon** | Turquoise | Turquoise | Shows us how to be kind with our words and actions. Answers our prayers and assists us with spiritual integrity. |

| Uriel | Pale yellow | Amber | Intellectual pursuits and how to solve problems. He illuminates our life path for us to follow. |
|---|---|---|---|
| **Zadkiel** | Indigo blue | Lapis lazuli | Helps with forgiveness and emotional clearing. |

# Spirit guides

Spirit guides are people who have had an earthly life but have passed over to the other side. They are here to help us with our spiritual growth. They have learned the lessons, so to speak, on the earth plane and have reached a high spiritual level, where they feel the need to help and assist others on the earth plane. Having experienced life's journey on earth they know how hard it can be at times. They are here to help us on our pathway but, like angels, they can (and will only) help when we ask for their assistance. They can help in whatever way is needed, a bit like a best friend, but one can only see them if very developed spiritually.

Many who are already in contact with them are unaware that they are! Such people as these have a little guiding voice inside them that they follow when they need guidance. This is in fact their spirit guide. Most just accept it as normal and follow its guidance, which is great, but others who hear the little voice ignore it! You may think you are going nuts when you hear it but trust me you are not; it is just a little help from above. So trust it when the messages that come through are loving and giving good guidance. If, however, the messages are more ego based and say things that don't ring true for you, then think before you act on its 'wisdom'.

Like old, wise mentors, spirit guides offer us advice when asked. They never judge us on our decisions in life but will offer us guidance when needed. Whether we take their advice is up to us. If we ask for advice but don't follow it, they will not judge us but will merely wait like a patient parent for the next task we ask of them. They are usually related to us or are someone that was close to us when they were alive, although this is not always the case. Our guide can change as we develop spiritually. We may start out with one guide and then find, after a few months, it has changed to another. This is because spirit guides come in different levels of development. They also have spiritual growth on the other side. They will take us to the level of their development and then another guide will take us to the next level.

We can speak to our guides like we would to a friend. They will answer our questions with either impressions of the right way to go, feelings of what we should do, quiet voices whispering into our ears or loud ones, flashes of images or symbols, or ideas in our dream state. We all obtain our guidance differently so go with what feels right for you. You may start out with an impression of the answer but later hear the guidance as you develop more spiritually. I heard my guidance the first time very loudly! It scared the life out of me because I wasn't expecting it to sound as if someone was in the room. I had imagined it would be a gentle voice, so be warned!!

Sometimes we can have naughty spirits that like to pretend to be our guides. They like to cause mischief and can try to lead us astray. So always check that you feel happy with the guidance that comes through. If it doesn't feel right ignore it and ask again on another day. You can also challenge any guide and ask, as below, if they are of the highest light. They have to give you a truthful answer.

"I ask you in the name of the Divine creator and the Holy

Spirit are you of the highest and purest of light?"

Ask this question three times and ask for a yes or no answer. Listen carefully for the answer and follow your instinct. If in doubt stop the contact and leave until another day. Never force contact with your guide if you can't 'hear' their answer; relax and try again at a later time. Sometimes when we try to force things to happen we actually block the connection. Working actively with our guides can take time and practice so if you don't have any impressions the first few times don't despair just keep at it and one day you will connect.

# Ascended masters

I will add a bit about these as they can also be very helpful. Ascended masters are people who have lived a mortal life and learned all of the lessons needed, to obtain a high vibration of energy. They have reached the higher levels where they don't need to return to this earthly plane. They are usually discussed in more depth in spiritual circles but I will add them here in the simplest form I can.

They are great healers, teachers and prophets who have come from all religions, cultures and civilizations throughout the world. They are such known figures as Buddha, Jesus, Saints, Goddesses and Gods.

We can ask for their help at any time. Like our guardian angels, they are happy to help, but we must first ask! You can ask out loud or quietly in your head. You don't have to believe in them for them to help you. They will help if you ask, but you must believe that a solution is possible and will be found somehow by someone!

**Abundantia** – attracts abundance into your life.

**Athena** – resolves arguments and attains justice.

**Babaji** – overcomes or reduces addictions and cravings.

**Brigit** – increases courage.

**Buddha** – helps spiritual growth and brings internal peace and harmony.

**El Morya** – helps with decision making.

**Isolt** – helps to heal after breakups, divorces or separations from a partner.

**Jesus** – helps with healing of all kinds and can bring miracles into our life.

**Kuan Yin** – helps the development of our spiritual gifts.

**Mother Mary** – can help with any child-related issues.

**Merlin** – can help with alchemy and divine magic.

**Moses** – can help to increase our courage and faith.

**Saint Francis** – can help us to find our life purpose.

**Saint John of God** – can soothe anxiety and depression and help us to find more joy in life.

**Saint Padre Pio** – can help us with forgiveness issues and help to heal the wounds left by it.

**Sanat Kumara** – can help us to dissolve and overcome ego issues, which affect our life.

**Serapis Bay** – motivates us to exercise and lose weight.

**Vywamus** – helps us to uncover our talents.

Above are just a few ascended masters who can help us. You could write their names down and keep the list by your bed or on your altar to draw them near to you and invoke them daily. Ask simply, for the help you need, and leave the solution to them, rather than tell them what you want to happen. The simpler the request the easier it is to interpret the answer, otherwise we over-complicate things and lose sight of the basic appeal. They will know far better than we how to resolve and help the problem as they see everything from the highest view point.

After asking, let the situation go and have faith that they will be helping you behind the scenes, so to speak. Keep them in your heart and just thank them daily, for helping you with your problem. Even if you can't see any immediate result don't stress; they will be helping resolve it as quickly as possible. Your thanking them, daily, will be sending out a powerful message to the universe that you know they are helping you. Give them a try because they are sure to surprise you...in the best way possible of course!!

# Colour Therapy

Colour is something that most of us take for granted. We are surrounded by it and its effects, but few of us acknowledge it. We wake up in the morning throw open our wardrobe and drag out the first garment that comes to hand …or do we? What if, on a deeper level, our subconscious mind was guiding us to the colour we needed for that day? Well, in reality, that is what happens. Colours do affect how we feel. Some people are always drawn to the same colours. They are sometimes even known by the colour they wear...such as a friend of mine who is called purple Annie. She always wears purple, sometimes even down to her shoes! I am also known for my leaning towards purple…purple glasses, hair and usually clothes!

Colours do have an enormous impact on how we are feeling. How many times do you hear expressions such as 'red' with anger, 'green' with envy, in a 'black' mood, feeling 'blue' and 'white' as a sheet? Colour is energy and, as such, it too carries a vibration or frequency. Each colour possesses a different frequency. It therefore has the power to calm, excite, inspire, balance, manipulate, induce a harmonic state and most importantly it can heal.

## So what exactly is colour?

Colour is light. It is light that is broken down into wave lengths, each wavelength vibrating at a different frequency or length. The different colours we see around us are caused by the light waves being absorbed or reflected off objects. Without light, there is no colour. Dark objects will absorb more light and reflect less light, whilst objects that look light will absorb less light and reflect more back.

Colour can be broken down into the three primary colours. These colours make up all the other colours that exist. This is shown below.

**Primary colours** – There are three primary colours.

**Red**
**Blue**
**Yellow**

**Secondary colours** – If two of these colours are mixed together they create a secondary colour.

**Violet** = red and blue
**Green** = blue and yellow
**Orange** = red and yellow

**Tertiary colours** – A tertiary colour is made when you mix a primary colour with a secondary colour.

**Turquoise** = blue and green
**Olive** = yellow and green
**Gold** = yellow and orange
**Coral** = red and orange
**Magenta** = red and violet
**Royal Blue** = blue and violet

**Complementary colours** – Each colour has its own complementary or contrasting colour. On a colour wheel it will be the opposite colour. Yellow is the complementary colour of violet because they are opposite each other on the colour wheel. Complementary colours can be used to calm their counterparts. For example, if you have a lot of the characteristics of yellow then you could wear the colour violet to help tone the yellow traits down as they are opposites on the colour wheel.

# Colour wheel

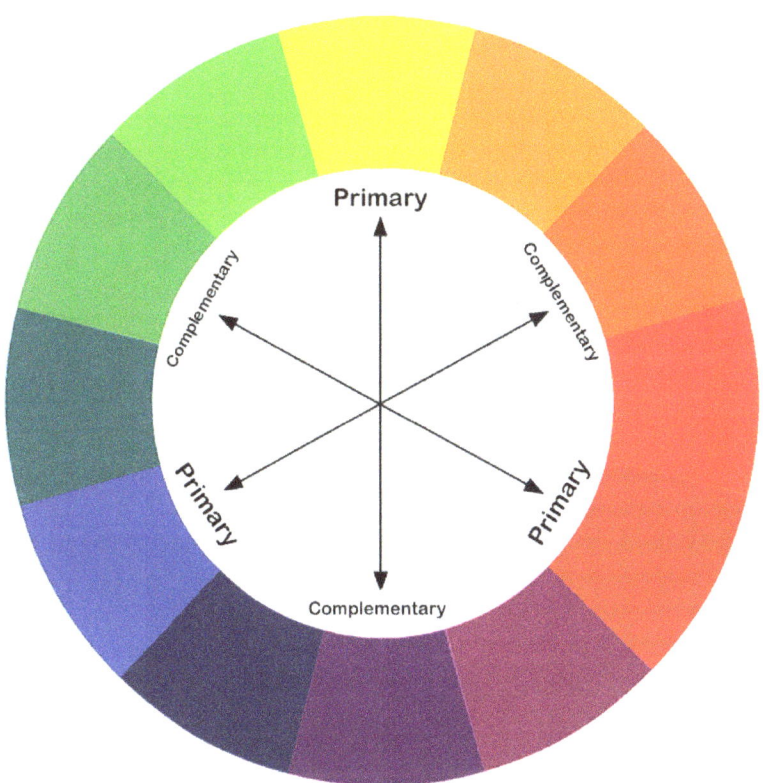

**Warm and cool colours** – On the colour wheel the warm colours are those that run from red through orange and yellow. These are energising, warming and happy colours. Cool colours are those that run from green through blue and violet. They tend to be calming, cooling and soothing.

# Characteristics of the colours

Each colour has a complementary colour. It also has certain characteristics that heighten both positive and negative aspects. Listed below are the positive and negative characteristics of each of the colours. The primary and secondary colours are related to the chakras of the body as they were. I have to say *'as they were'* because, after 2012, the chakra systems began to change colour, as new chakras of higher frequencies were being integrated into the body.

Our bodies intuitively know what colours we are lacking and will draw us to those colours. How often have you been drawn to a particular colour such as red when you are feeling low on energy or green when you are feeling 'under the weather'? You might find your colour choices changing with the seasons or with certain periods of your life. While I was going through my traumatic divorce I was drawn to wear green and pink. This represented my need to be balanced with the green ray and loved with the pink ray. At others times I was drawn to wear grounding colours of browns.

If we begin to observe what colours draw us to them, it can tell us a lot about how we are really feeling. It is time for us to listen to our bodies and give them what they need. Colours can also be used consciously when we know which areas need help and/or healing. When we lack clear thinking, we could wear yellow to boost our concentration and help us focus. Adding colour to our life is a simple way to help us on our journey of self-discovery and healing.

# Red

Associated with the base chakra.

Turquoise is the complementary colour of red.

Red is strong, powerful, dominating– a colour of stability and security. It is vibrant and energising and will stimulate the body into action. It will bring passion into your life to bolster you up, enabling you to see all the beauty around you. It boosts self-esteem and enthusiasm. If you are one whose motivation wanes from time to time, especially when having to do a job you dread, then red will give you the lift that is needed to get the job done. It will also boost desire if your libido is waning – hence red lingerie always being sold for Valentine's Day!

Physically, it is comforting when feeling tired or cold, or suffer from poor circulation, are anaemic or have low blood pressure. Sexual and fertility problems are helped by passionate red. Lower-back problems are also helped as well as feelings of loneliness or insecurity.

**Do not use** when feeling angry or hyperactive as these problems will be heightened by passionate red, as would heart problems or high blood pressure. Also avoid red when relaxing because it will vitalise your energy not calm it!

# Orange

Associated with the sacral chakra.

Blue is the complementary colour of orange.

It is warm and assertive but is not as intense as red. It contains both the red and yellow rays. Therefore, it will have the passion of red and the intellect of yellow. It is a colour of joy and optimism. Like red, it is good for when you are feeling tired but too much can over-stimulate and cause tiredness and confusion. It has a direct relationship with the adrenal glands, which are our 'energy' powerhouses. When you are feeling 'blue', or depressed, then orange is a good colour to bring more joy into your life. It is good for when one feels inhibited or indecisive about which way to go in life.

It works directly on one's emotions paving the way to a happier, brighter, more contented you. Communication skills are improved, breaking down barriers and awakening one's inner potential and creativity. Too much orange can bring on boredom, listlessness and even sadness.

Physically it helps to energise the adrenal glands. Working on the genito-urinary system, it boosts the liver by aiding detoxification and it aids the appetite. The metabolism is stimulated along with the immune system. It also helps boost the libido and can help with menstrual problems, cramps, asthma and indigestion.

**Do not use** when you are feeling angry or irritable as the red ray will enhance these feelings, nor if you have digestive problems, feel nauseous or you have a tendency to overeat. Also avoid if you are suffering from incontinence.

## Yellow

Associated with the solar plexus chakra.

Its complementary colour is violet.

After white, yellow is the closest to the light of the sun in brightness and hue. This warming, cheerful colour will boost your concentration, stimulate intellectual ability and enhance mental clarity. This is because yellow is associated with the intellect, the left or logical side of the brain. Use it for opening you up to new ideas and illuminating the mind. It removes negative thoughts, making it a good aid when studying or doing written work. When your memory or decision-making skills are poor, then bring on the yellow. Yellow is a colour of confidence, great to use when you are feeling nervous. It will revitalise flagging spirits, but too much will overexcite and make concentration difficult.

Physically, it improves poor digestion, alleviates constipation, diabetes, the adrenal glands, nervous system, skin problems, and the circulatory system.

**Do not use** when aggression or hyperactivity is a problem as it will be too stimulating. It will also be too stimulating when you are feeling stressed, suffer from insomnia or if you suffer from an over-active digestive system.

## Green

Associated with the heart chakra.

Its complementary colour is magenta.

Green is a cooling, relaxing colour. It is the colour of nature and balance. When we feel stressed, nature is usually our first port of call to clear our heads. Use it when you feel that your emotions or lifestyle are out of balance. Green calms the emotions and brings facts back into focus after an argument. It is a healing, harmonious colour, promoting love, compassion, sensitivity and peace. It is a good colour for helping to reduce anxiety. It must be noted however that too much green may make you feel unmotivated or lethargic.

Physically, it helps to energise the thymus gland and boost a low immune system. It stimulates the lungs and can help with breathing problems. Helpful for claustrophobia, flu, heart problems, high blood pressure, arthritis, and allergies.

**Do not use** when you have an auto-immune condition.

## Pale Blue

Associated with the throat chakra.

Its complementary colour is red.

This cool colour denotes peacefulness, trust and faithfulness. It stimulates communication and self-expression. When you are feeling ill-at-ease, or stressed, blue will cool and relax you with its peaceful energies. Too much, however, can cause apathy and melancholy. Physically, it stimulates the thyroid gland, controls high blood pressure, menstrual and hearing problems and slows the metabolism. It is good for any hot or inflammatory conditions such as burns, eczema, fevers, headaches, psoriasis, rheumatism, sunburn and swollen glands.

**Do not use** when the immune system is sluggish and you feel a tightness in the body, have thyroid deficiency or if you feel the cold.

## Indigo

Associated with the third eye chakra.

Its complementary colour is orange.

This is the colour of heightened awareness. It stimulates the brain and enhances our imagination and creativity. If you are lacking in inspiration, or can't think clearly, bring on indigo. It also enhances your intuition and is good when you have feelings of restlessness or are agitated. Too much indigo can leave you feeling ungrounded and empty.

Physically, helps the pineal gland, deafness, haemorrhage, insomnia, migraine, central nervous system, and hormonal activity.

**Do not use** when you are feeling depressed, suffer from SAD disorder, have menstrual problems or are suffering from nightmares.

## Violet

Associated with the crown chakra.

Its complementary colour is yellow.

Violet is associated with spirituality, it is a colour of dignity and self-respect. Using violet will help you to connect to your more spiritual side, thus encouraging fulfilment, commitment and contentment. It is a good colour to use when you have lost faith in yourself and don't appreciate yourself enough. It brings more purpose and meaning to life. It is a good colour to use while meditating or with visualisation. Too much violet, however, can lead to foolish pride and arrogance.

Physically it helps: concussion, epilepsy, neuralgia, multiple sclerosis and the pituitary gland.

**Do not use** if suffering from serious psychological or mental problems, or addictions.

## Other colours of interest in healing.

<u>**Turquoise**</u> – a mix of blue and green that combines the qualities of both the serenity of blue and the harmony of green. Turquoise is a calming colour for both the physical body and the emotions. It is a great colour to wear if you have to speak publically, because it is calming and will enhance your communication skills. It helps you to speak from the heart, to say what you really mean and feel.

Physically, it helps any inflammatory conditions, colds, flu, burns, wounds, and it boosts the immune system.

**Magenta** – a mix of red and violet that combines the qualities of both the passion of red and the transcendence of violet. Magenta helps us to let-go of the old and embrace the new. It is the colour of change, the releasing of the old, outworn patterns and habits. It is a calming, soothing colour, good for stabilising those who tend to be emotionally volatile, aggressive or violent.

Physically, it helps to energise the adrenal glands, kidneys, and acts as a diuretic.

**Brown** – a grounding colour. It connects our feet firmly to Mother earth. It is good to use when we are feeling spaced out, or disconnected with what's going on around us. It has a steadying influence, which helps us to stay on the straight and narrow. Brown helps to concentrate our energies on the task in hand, rather than dissipating them in all directions. It is a colour associated with reliability and down-to-earth common sense. It is a good colour when you feel you are at the mercy of external influences, and feel the need to protect yourself. However, too much brown can make you feel afraid to embrace changes in your life.

**Black** – although not a colour, as such, because it absorbs all the rays of the light spectrum, it is still worth mentioning. Although it has many negative connotations such as being a 'funeral' colour, black sheep of the family, black magic …it does have some positives as well. We say our bank balance is 'in the black' and seeing a black cat is good luck. Black is a colour of power and control. It speaks of dignity and discretion. When we wear a black suit it makes us feel more powerful, making it a good choice for interviews or when facing your opposition! Black is the colour of protection and is a good colour to wear when feeling vulnerable.

**White** – again, white is not a colour, as such, because it is all colours reflected. White is symbolic of goodness and purity. It is a colour of positivity because it reflects all the colours back to us. It is very spiritual, helping us to feel more connected to our higher selves, especially when used with violet. Too much white can indicate that we feel the colour has gone out of our life.

# How to use colour in your life for healing

## Wearing colour

We can choose to wear the colours we need every day. This is one of the simplest ways to benefit. We probably already have the colours needed among the clothes we have because we are often drawn to them when shopping. This is our intuition taking over and drawing us to the colours that we need.

Our taste in colours can change from season to season depending on what we need at that time. If we are feeling very emotional we will be drawn to the gentle calming colour of blue, or if we feel spaced out with our head floating in the clouds then brown will help to ground us. If you suffer from that Monday morning lack of energy, then red will give you a boost while yellow will help you step out into your day with confidence.

If you have to wear a uniform and are unable to wear the colours you need, then buy underwear in those colours. That way you can still benefit from them during the day. This is also a good option if you need to wear a colour that doesn't suit your complexion. There is nothing worse than having to wear something that doesn't suit you or makes you look drained because it clashes with your skin colour. 'T' shirts are another good way of adding colour, especially in the winter, when you can wear them under a jumper so that they aren't seen! When you find you are drawn to colours differing from normal, go with the flow and listen to what your body is telling you. It is usually right, but we rarely trust it! It can be very exhilarating to do so!

## Using coloured water

Another simple way of applying colour to the body is to use solarised water. Water, when placed in a coloured container and exposed to sunlight, will absorb the vibrational energy of that colour. This can then be drunk or used for bathing a particular part of the body to bring about healing.

To make solarised water you will need:
- A clean, plain glass
- A coloured light-filter (obtainable from the internet)
- An elastic band
- Pure, still, mineral water
- Kitchen towel

1. Attach the light-filter to the glass using the elastic band.
2. Fill the glass with the mineral water, then cover with the kitchen towel.

3. Place on a window sill.

4. Leave for a minimum of two hours, or longer if the sun is not very bright!

5. The water can be kept in the refrigerator and will last 5 days.

6. The water can be sipped throughout the day.

Remember that the red, orange and yellow waters will be stimulating so don't drink these too late in the day or they will keep you awake at night. Whereas, the blue, indigo and violet are calming and are best drunk in the latter part of the day. Any problem areas such as acne can be bathed with the water to treat the area.

## Colour table for physical dis-ease

| COLOUR | BENEFITS |
|---|---|
| Red | Chilblains can be bathed with the water. Re-energise the body in the morning ready for the day ahead. Helps raise low blood pressure. Boosts a slow circulation. |
| Orange | Depression. Digestive problems. Menstrual problems and period pains. Cramps and muscular spasms. |
| Yellow | Aids concentration so is good to use when studying. Has a laxative and diuretic property. Stabilises weight– drink a glass 30mins before eating. Helps combat urine infections. |
| Green | Lowers high blood pressure. Strengthens the immune system. |
| Blue | Anti-inflammatory and anti-septic. Helps relieve stings, itches and rashes. Calms a fever. Helps thyroid imbalances. Comforts teething babies. Gargle the water to help relieve sore throats. |
| Indigo | Purifies the blood and helps varicose veins. Treats boils, ulcers, shingles, chicken pox and measles. Gives pain-relief and treats rheumatism and arthritis. Heals wounds and eczema by drinking the water and bathing the area. |
| Violet | Purifies and calms the body. Treats nervous headaches and migraines. Skin, acne – as well as drinking the water, scarring can be bathed. Psoriasis of the scalp can be relieved by bathing. |
| Turquoise (blue & green benefits as well) | Energises the thyroid. Heals the emotions. Boosts the immune system. |
| Magenta (red & violet benefits as well) | Energises the body. Treats skin complaints by bathing the problem-area with the water. |

## Coloured silks

Coloured silks can be laid on the body to induce more colour into any of the chakras that are out of balance. It is best to wear pure white when applying the coloured silks to an area. Lie down, ensuring that you are in a comfortable position. Then simply place the coloured silk over the chakra that is out of balance. Relax for at least 30mins so the chakra can absorb the colour or colours. More than one silk can be applied. For a complete body balance each chakra can be treated at the same time.

Coloured silks can be obtained from the internet.

## Colour breathing

Colours can be visualised when breathing to bring a quick 'fix' of colour when you need it. They can give us an instant boost when we don't have the colour we need to hand. It is simple to do… All you need is your imagination!

### Colour breathing technique

- Stand with your feet a little way apart and relax.
- Relax each muscle from your head down to your feet.
- Allow your arms to hang loosely by your side.
- Now imagine, before you, a cloud of your chosen colour.
- Slowly bring this colour into your body on the inhale.
- Imagine it moving to the chakra that is out of balance

- Imagine the breath finding your bodily problems.

- As you exhale, breathe the problems out of the body.

- Continue to do this for a few minutes until you start to feel the effect of the colour on the body. If you are breathing in 'red' for example you should start to feel more energised.

- Continue until you intuitively feel you have done enough.

- Now gently bring your awareness back to the present. Gently stamp your feet, grounding you down again.

This breathing exercise can be done in the morning to revitalise the body using the stimulating colours – red, orange and yellow or, at night, to relax the body using the calming colours – blue, violet and green.

## Colour breathing for mental well-being

Our emotions can be brought into balance quickly by using colour-breathing. This technique can be used anywhere at any time to bring quick relief. Use the table below to find the colour that matches what you would like to bring into your life more: energy, peace, calm, confidence etc. and then colour-breathe as described above, with your chosen colour. If you need more than one colour, then alternate the colours each time you practice colour-breathing. Or use the energising colours in the morning and the calming colours in the evening.

## Colour table for mental and emotional dis-ease

| COLOUR | PROMOTES |
|---|---|
| Red | Enhances courage and confidence. Is energising and aids will power. Is motivating and strengthening on the body. Assists one's attention to detail. |
| Orange | Stimulates and revitalises the mind and body. Enhances self-esteem and inner strength, promoting a more optimistic outlook on life. It aids creativity and self-expression, and helps open the mind to new ideas. Promotes happiness. |
| Yellow | Uplifting and mentally stimulating. Enhances self-confidence and self-respect. It promotes more self-control by aiding your ability to rationalise and reason, which, in turn, brings more contentment into one's life. |
| Green | A balancing colour of nature bringing a sense of harmony. Helps personal development and self-acceptance and enhances compassion for one's self and others. |
| Blue | Calming and peaceful, this aids relaxation, bringing inner balance to the self. Aids self-expression, creativity and enhances our intuition. Promotes honesty and truth. |
| Indigo | Promotes our inner wisdom and intuition and aids us on our spiritual path.<br>It brings more understanding of the self. Promotes peace and calm and enhances our inspiration. |
| Violet | Enhances our inspiration and imagination. This empathic colour aids our sense of belonging, promoting self-respect and dignity. |
| Turquoise (blue & green benefits as well) | Promotes inner calm, enhances our resilience and aids healing. Helps with personal relationships, friendships and sharing and aids our communication. |

| | |
|---|---|
| **Magenta (red & violet benefits as well)** | Assists us in letting go of the past, helps us release anxious thoughts and encourages us to move on in life. Aids our spiritual understanding and growth. |
| **Pink** | Calming and loving, this enhances our clarity of thought, promotes affection, compassion, nurturing and kindness. |
| **Gold** | Enhances our enthusiasm and balances our thoughts and feelings to align with our inner wisdom. |

## Meditating with colour

Meditation is a form of relaxation. It involves shutting down the mental chatter that is constantly going on inside our head and allows us to relax. It is a time of contemplation where we can give ourselves the time and space needed to connect with our higher wisdom.

We live in hectic, busy times where it is the norm to rush around and never have any quiet time. We think we don't have the time for contemplation because we 'have so much to do'. What few people realise is that when we are constantly busy we begin to work on autopilot and lose our mental clarity. This loss of clarity can lead us down the wrong path in life, it can create no end of stressful situations and causes the body to work overtime, which will eventually lead to illness.

By making quiet time we are helping the body and mind to combat these potential problems. When I say quiet time I don't mean sitting in front of the TV either! This pursuit may feel relaxing but it can over-stimulate the brain so that sleep becomes more difficult. It does take a little time to 'master' meditation but it is worth the effort. The results will have a profound effect on your health physically and mentally. It is like anything new, practice makes perfect!

## Meditating with coloured silks

First choose a time you know you will not be disturbed. Choosing to meditate at the same time each day will help, because the body will grow used to this. If you can't, then don't worry. Now, choose a coloured silk to work with or if you feel drawn to more than one choose the one that drew you first. Then when you meditate again you can use the other colour. Coloured cotton or other material can be used if you don't want to go to the expense of obtaining silk. Silk is just such a lovely soft tactile natural fabric. This might be a colour matching a chakra that is out of balance, able to help you relax or energise you, or just choose one that you are drawn to. Remember your body always knows what's best for it so trust in it.

Find a place that is warm and comfortable, making sure there will be no distractions– out of the window for example!

Make sure your chair is comfortable and relaxing. You should be sitting with a relatively straight back, if possible.

Ensure that anything needing to be done is sorted before you meditate or you will sit thinking about what you have to do instead of quieting the mind!

Play soft music in the background to help you to relax.

Light a candle to mark the start of the meditation. This will trigger the body to know it is time to relax. Little rituals like this soon become habits, which will help you relax more quickly each time.

Sit quietly and begin to relax the body.

Start to breathe in through the nose and out through the nose. Place your hands on your tummy and feel the breath from there. This will ensure your breath is coming from the diaphragm and not from chest, ensuring a deep cleansing breath rather than a shallow one.

Breathe consciously in and out. On breathing in, breathe in the feelings of peace. Feel or imagine, that peace, filling the body. You can just imagine the word being breathed in, go with whatever feels natural to you. Don't worry if it feels difficult at first. Just persevere. Soon it will become easier.

Now when you breathe out, breathe out any tension in the body. You can imagine the word or just feel it leaving you.

Continue to breathe *in* peace and *out* tension. Do this for as long as feels natural, for the body to begin to relax.

If any mental chatter enters your mind just let it gently float away. Don't stress about the mental chatter just imagine putting it in a bucket and letting it go.

Continue to relax and quiet the mind.
Gently open your eyes and focus on the coloured cloth of your choice. Hold it in your hands and really focus on the colour. Feel the colour gently flowing into the body and balancing any areas that need help. Sit holding and 'playing' with the coloured cloth for as long as you feel you need to. A minimum of 20mins would be ideal, but if you want to relax for longer that would be even more beneficial. If, at any point, you feel like holding the cloth to a particular part of the body go ahead. Do what your intuition guides you to do. However, never wrap any cloth around the neck area. If you feel you need colour here, then drape over one shoulder or hold to the front of the neck.

Once you feel you have absorbed enough colour slowly bring your awareness back to the present moment. Rubbing your hands along your thighs can help bring you back faster as it will help to ground you. Stretch gently.

You are now ready to face the world with a renewed energy.

Meditation is renowned for helping multiple health problems. It is worthwhile practicing the habit. If you can only manage 10mins a day, that is still beneficial. However, once you feel the benefits you will usually 'make' time to meditate more each day, and may find that you extend your time to an hour!

Helpful for: emotional wellbeing, raising your awareness, concentration, anxiety, asthma, breathing difficulties, chronic pain, circulatory problems, headaches, high blood pressure, insomnia, migraines, muscular aches and pains, and any stress related problems.

## Visualisation with colour

Colour visualisation is another great way to bring more colour into your life. It's also great for stimulating your imagination. Visualisation is similar to meditation but it involves creating pictures with the mind. Some people find this easier than others but, as with meditation, the more you practice the easier it becomes.

### Visualisation with colour 1

- Find a comfortable place with no distractions.
- Sit as upright as possible in a comfortable chair.
- Sort what needs to be done before starting.
- Play some soft music to help you to relax.
- Light a candle to match the colour you visualise. Focus on it until you relax and close your eyes.
- Breathe in and out, feel the breath from your stomach rather than the chest.

- Imagine peace filling the body.
- Imagine the tension leaving you.
- Do this until the body to begins to relax.
- Don't stress about the mental chatter.
- Continue to relax and quiet the mind.
- Visualise the colour that you want to work with.
- See the colour building like a gentle cloud in front of you. See it expand outwards until it is big enough to cover your body. Now see yourself stepping into this cloud of colour. See it swirling around you. Feel the colour entering the body and imagine it going to where it is needed. Let your mind drift as the colour enters different parts of the body. Feel the effect the colour has on you. It may energise you if it is a stimulating colour or it may help relax you.
- Gently sit with this colourful cloud for as long as you feel you need it. A minimum of 20mins would be ideal, but if you want to relax for longer that will be even more beneficial.
- Once you feel you have absorbed enough colour see the cloud gently drifting away from you and dissolving away. Now slowly bring your awareness back to the present moment. Rubbing your hands along your thighs can help bring you back faster as it will help to ground you. Slowly open your eyes and stretch gently.
- You are now ready to face the world with a renewed energy.

## Visualisation with colour 2

Follow the above to relax the body, continue to relax and quiet the mind part.

Now imagine yourself sat in a beautiful garden. You are surrounded by flowers.

Imagine yourself gently get up from your comfortable chair and go to take a closer look at some of the flowers. The grass is soft underfoot. The birds are singing and the gentle sun brushes your skin with warmth.

The first flower you see is a bright red rose. As you focus on the flower it gently opens wide to reveal its inner beauty. Gaze softly at the rose and absorb its energising red colour feel it enter your base chakra. When you feel you have had your fill of red move on to the next flower.

This time it is a group of orange marigolds. Again, as you gaze at their beauty the flowers open fully to reveal the tiny petals at the centre. Feel the orange enter your sacral chakra filling your tummy with a warm glow. Absorb the beauty and colour before moving onto the next flower.

Tall regal sunflowers stand before you next. Slowly they turn towards you to reveal their golden yellow. They stand proud full of confidence. Feel this confidence entering your solar plexus.

As you move on again, you come across some beautiful pink roses. These too open beneath your gaze. Revealing their soft pink. This pink is gentle and loving and enters your heart filling it with love.

Now you come across some pale blue forget me not's. These pale blue tiny flowers glow before your eyes revealing their beauty. They gently pour their pale blue colour into the throat, opening it and relaxing it. Communication comes easier to you now.

Next is a deep indigo rose. This rose is as dark as the night sky. As you stare into its depths you see the wonders of the universe before your eyes. Twirling stars bring you knowledge. Lose yourself in this swirling beauty as this universal knowledge enters your brow chakra.

Next is a lilac bush. It is full of blooms of tiny flowers. They bow down to you as they fill your crown chakra with violet colour.

Now you see a tiny path leading to a pergola with a seating area. You stroll towards it, and gently climb the seven steps. With each step you will feel lighter, more relaxed.

Sit quietly and relax in the beautiful surroundings. This is special place with healing powers that can help you with anything that you need guidance on. State your question clearly and wait for an answer. Sometimes we are given answer in the form of words before our eyes, sometimes symbols that mean something to us, or we may hear the answer. Whatever comes to you, take note of it. If you find nothing comes to you don't worry it may come at a later date or in your dream state.

When you feel ready make your way back down the seven steps. Past the flowers and return to your seat in the garden.

Gently bring your awareness back to the present. Rub your thighs to help ground you and gently stretch.

These are just two examples of different styles of colour visualisation. You can start with these as guides but please feel free to adapt them to what suits you best.

## Eating colour

Fresh fruit and vegetables come in a multiple of colours. Think of a ruby-red apple. How do we feel after eating it? Usually better and more energised! This is not just because of the nutrients of the apple but also because we have taken in a blast of vibrant red energy! When we are feeling tired and unable to concentrate how many of us reach for a banana? The slow release of fruit-sugars gives us more energy, while its yellow colour boosts our concentration.

How balanced is your diet, colour-wise? The next time you prepare a meal, note the colours you are using. Is there one colour you favour? Do you miss some colours completely from your diet? If you feel under-the-weather, do you always reach for the same food? If so what is the colour?

By asking yourself questions like these you can work out if you are taking in all the colours. If you are missing some, do the colours correspond to any of the chakras that you know are out of balance? If so, you can rectify this by introducing the missing colours into your diet.

If possible, try to buy organic fruit and vegetables. They are so much better for the body with more nutrients than their supermarket equivalents. They also have more flavour and you may find you enjoy eating more!

## Red, orange and yellow

These stimulating foods energise the body, cleansing and purifying the blood and boosting our immune system. They are grounding foods that anchor us to the physical plane of existence giving us the energy to stay focused in the physical world, so that we may interact positively with life.

Red foods contain iron, which is used in the formation of red blood cells and keeps our energy levels up.

Orange foods contain vitamin C, which is needed for overall health.

Yellow food is needed for a healthy digestive system. It helps to detoxify the body, supporting the nervous system and the mental processes (concentration, memory, reasoning etc.).

| **RED FOODS** |
|---|
| Red meat (eat small portions as it is high in fat) |
| Beetroot, Kidney beans, Leafy dark green vegetables (high in iron so they qualify), Red cabbage/chillies/peppers, tomatoes |
| Black/White pepper, Cayenne pepper, Ginger, Red sage, Rosemary |
| Apples, Cherries, Plums, Raspberries, Redcurrants, Rhubarb, Strawberries |

| **ORANGE FOODS** |
|---|
| Egg yolks, Orange lentils |
| Butternut Squash, Carrots, Orange peppers, Pumpkin, Squash, Swede, Turnip |
| Coriander seeds, Cumin |
| Apricots, Mangoes, Melons, Nectarines, Oranges, Pawpaw's, Peaches, Satsuma's, Tangerines |

| **YELLOW FOODS** |
|---|
| Butter(in moderation!), Nuts, Oils, Seeds, Whole grains, Yellow lentils |
| Squash, Sweet corn, Yellow peppers |
| Caraway, Cinnamon, Dill, Lemon grass, Saffron |
| Bananas, Grapefruit, Lemons, Pineapples |

*Red, orange and yellow are warming and invigorating.*

## Green

Green is the colour of nature and green foods promote a healthy body. They are full of vitamins and minerals to keep our body and energy levels in balance. These should be eaten daily and in abundance! Green is the colour of the heart chakra so it's not surprising that many green foods help promote a healthy heart function. Green foods contain vitamin C and beta-carotene, which help prevent heart disease.

Green foods also alleviate headaches, lower blood pressure, relieve stress and soothe the emotions.

| GREEN FOODS |
| --- |
| Green lentils, Yoghurt, Tofu |
| Artichokes, Asparagus, Avocado, Broccoli, Cabbage, Celery, Courgettes, Cucumber, Green beans, Green peppers, Lettuce, Peas, Watercress |
| Alfalfa, Basil, Chervil, Chives, Coriander leaves, Mint, Parsley, Tarragon |
| Apples, Grapes, Greengages, Gooseberries, Kiwi fruit, Limes, Pears |

***Green food is full of vitamins and minerals needed for a healthy balanced body.***

### Blue, indigo and violet foods

There is not such an abundance of blue, indigo or violet foods as there is with the other colours but it still forms an important part of our diet. These colours are the opposite of the red, orange and yellow foods and are therefore cooling and calming on the body. These colours nourish the brain, higher mental faculties and the nervous system.

| BLUE, INDIGO and VIOLET FOODS |
| --- |
| Black beans, Black soybeans |
| Aubergines, Black olives, Mushrooms, Purple broccoli, Purple-leaved lettuce, Seaweed |
| Blue sage, Juniper berries, Purple basil |
| Bilberries, Blackberries, Blueberries, Black cherries, Currants, Prunes, Raisins |

***Blue, Indigo and Violet foods are great for cooling, calming and inspiration.***

# Altars

Altars are a great way to use your creative abilities to construct a visual focus point where you can work on chakras. The altar would be your own sacred space, serving as a visual daily reminder of the Chakra needing attention.

We can use them for a daily ritual. Rituals have been used for centuries to bring psychological comfort; they have a steadying effect. Grounding is a useful tool these days, as we always seem to be on the run from one thing to another and rarely feel the calming stability of just standing still!

Once you have decided which chakra needs to be worked on, you can create your own altar to use as a daily focal point for your mind. You can attend to your altar daily or even twice daily to absorb the colours and quiet the mind. They can be excellent places for meditation and a daily ritual will enable your mind to relax and be more open to hearing the messages that your body is trying to tell you.

So what do you put on your altar?

- Coloured cloth or ribbons to match the colour of your chakra.
- Coloured candles to match the colour of your chakra.
- Crystals associated with the chakra.
- Crystals associated with dis-ease.
- The Archetype and/or animal associated with the chakra.
- Flowers to match the colour of the chakra.
- Essential oil, Fragrance or incense that is associated with the chosen chakra.
- Pictures of the ruling planet and/or astrological sign associated with the chakra.

- Any item that is associated with the 'sense' that matches the chakra.
- Any coloured item that is meaningful to you that also matches the colour of the chakra.
- Any items relevant to the chakra being worked on. A strongly sentimental gift from a friend, for example, could be used on a heart chakra to help the heart centre open.
- Any item that you are drawn to place on the altar.

Remember it is your sacred space for you to decorate in any way that feels good for you. It is an expression of your creativity. You can have a large altar or a tiny altar the result will be the same! The contents may change, as they are removed when they no longer feel right and replaced with something else. You may find yourself rearranging things on your altar each day to create a different look. Again, just do what feels good for you!

If, after a while, you no longer want the colour you have chosen and feel the need to change it, this just means that you have worked sufficiently with the chakra of your choice and it is time to work on another one.

If unsure which chakra to work on first, then you can always start with the base chakra and work up to the crown chakra. Some altars may be with you for a longer period than others.

Just learn to go with the flow!

The following chart offers guidance about what to use on your altar according to the selected chakra.

## BASE/ROOT CHAKRA

| | |
|---|---|
| **Base/root chakra** | Located at the base of the spine |
| **Associated animals/archetypes** | Elephant. Earth Mother/victim |
| **Associated body parts** | Bones, skeleton |
| **Associated colour** | Red |
| **Associated sense** | Smell |
| **Astrological signs** | Capricorn |
| **Crystals** | Agate, bloodstone, hematite, obsidian, red jasper, smoky quartz, tigers eye |
| **Element** | Earth |
| **Fragrance** | Cedar wood, myrrh |
| **Ruling planet** | Saturn |

## SACRAL CHAKRA

| | |
|---|---|
| **Sacral chakra** | Located in the naval area |
| **Associated animals/archetypes** | Fish tailed alligator. Sovereign/martyr |
| **Associated body parts** | Bladder, ovaries & womb (female), prostate & testes (male) |
| **Associated colour** | Orange |
| **Associated sense** | Taste |
| **Astrological signs** | Cancer, Scorpio |
| **Crystals** | Amber, orange calcite, carnelian, citrine, golden topaz, moonstone, rutilated quartz |
| **Element** | Water |
| **Fragrance** | Jasmine, rose |
| **Ruling planet** | Pluto |

## SOLAR PLEXUS CHAKRA

| Solar plexus chakra | Located at the base of the sternum |
|---|---|
| Associated animals/archetypes | Ram. Spiritual warrior/drudge |
| Associated body parts | Digestive system, muscles |
| Associated colour | Yellow |
| Associated sense | Sight |
| Astrological signs | Aries, Leo |
| Crystals | Amber, aventurine, yellow/gold calcite, citrine, rutilated quartz, sunstone |
| Element | Fire |
| Fragrance | Bergamot, ylang ylang |
| Ruling planet | Mars, Sun |

## HEART CHAKRA

| | |
|---|---|
| **Heart chakra** | Located in the middle of the chest |
| **Associated animals/archetypes** | Gazelle. Lover/performer |
| **Assoc. body parts** | Circulation, heart, lungs |
| **Associated colour** | Green &/or pink |
| **Associated sense** | Touch |
| **Astrological signs** | Libra, Taurus |
| **Crystals** | Green aventurine, green calcite, emerald, rose quartz, rhodochrosite, rhodonite, ruby |
| **Element** | Air |
| **Fragrance** | Bergamot, rose |
| **Ruling planet** | Venus |

## THROAT CHAKRA

| | |
|---|---|
| **Throat chakra** | Located in the throat area |
| **Associated animals/archetypes** | Bull. Communicator/ masked self |
| **Associated body parts** | Ears, mouth, throat |
| **Associated colour** | Pale blue |
| **Associated sense** | Hearing |
| **Astrological signs** | Gemini, Virgo |
| **Crystals** | Aquamarine, azurite, blue lace agate, blue calcite, celestite, chrysocolla, kyanite, lapis lazuli, turquoise |
| **Element** | Ether |
| **Fragrance** | Chamomile, myrrh |
| **Ruling planet** | Mercury |

## THIRD EYE/BROW CHAKRA

| | |
|---|---|
| **Third eye chakra** | Located between the eyebrows |
| **Associated archetypes** | Psychic/ rationalist |
| **Associated body parts** | Eyes, base of skull |
| **Associated colour** | Indigo blue |
| **Associated sense** | Sixth sense |
| **Astrological signs** | Sagittarius, Pisces |
| **Crystals** | Amethyst, azurite, fluorite, kyanite, lapis lazuli, sodalite, sugilite |
| **Element** | Light |
| **Fragrance** | Hyacinth, rose geranium |
| **Ruling planet** | Jupiter, Neptune |

## CROWN CHAKRA

| | |
|---|---|
| **Crown chakra** | Located at the top of the head |
| **Associated archetypes** | Guru/ egocentric |
| **Associated body parts** | Cerebral cortex, upper skull, skin |
| **Associated colour** | Violet, white |
| **Associated sense** | Spiritual/ higher self |
| **Astrological signs** | Aquarius |
| **Crystals** | Amber, amethyst, apophylite, citrine, diamond, fluorite, Herkimer diamond, quartz, sugilite, gold topaz |
| **Element** | Universal energy |
| **Fragrance** | Frankincense, lavender |
| **Ruling planet** | Uranus |

These are the energies associated with each chakra. You can use some or all of the ideas to create your own altar. Where a smell is associated with the chakra you can use essential oils, or incense sticks, to draw the energies in. Where the elements are used, plants can be used for both air and earth and candles for fire, but only light them if you are present in the room. Sea salt crystals, as these are salt in its natural form, can also be used to represent the earth. Cut flowers can be added to give the element of water, or use a small fountain if you have one. The animals and archetypes can be taken from the internet and put in frames, or you could just write the names on cards and add them to your altar. Use your imagination and be drawn to what feels right for you. If it looks wrong, then change it until you have what feels and looks good to you.

Altars make lovely places to meditate at each day. They hold the colours and energies of the chakra you are working on. Every time you sit and meditate at your altar you will be building energy there. You may notice its peacefulness even when passing it, but take time to sit and to enjoy it. A few moments spent each day will bring huge benefits to your mind, body and soul!

# Altar examples

## Base/Root Chakra Altar

This vibrant altar will bring a blast of energy into your life. It represents our survival instincts. It shows someone wanting more security in their life. Any object can be added that represents what you feel you need in your life to feel more secure.

- A model car could be added if you feel that would give you the freedom you seek!

- Red candles with a drop of patchouli essential oil added when lit, represent the ability to smell.

- Hematite, bloodstone and tigers eye crystals are associated with the base chakra.

- Money and house keys represent security. They can be used to draw it to us if it is what we need.

- The two angels represent help from above. They can represent our guardian angel supporting us.

- The elephant figurine and pendant are the animal representation associated with the base chakra.
- The red silk represents the colour of the chakra.
- The rose represents the element of earth in its simplest form. A fresh rose would be better but artificial can be used if more convenient!

## Sacral Chakra Altar

This is a more elaborate altar. An area for quiet meditation and contemplation. It is a very feminine and spiritual altar designed to bring a sense of calm. There are a lot of spiritual elements in it. It represents someone looking for emotional balance by having trust in what the universe throws at us and knowing there is always a higher purpose to what we experience, be it good or bad!

- The Buddha representing emotional balance.
- The orange scarf representing the colour of the sacral chakra.
- The orange rose in water and the shells represent the element of water.
- The fish-tailed crocodile is the animal association represented by the figurine.
- The orange fruit represents the sense of taste, bringing more sweetness into our life.
- The flowers and pretty box represent the feminine side.
- The crystals are carnelian, orange calcite and citrine, associated with the sacral chakra.
- The bracelet was a special gift from a friend and fits in well being carnelian crystals.
- The lights, angel and candles represent bringing more light into life.

## Solar Plexus Chakra Altar

This altar is to represent someone who feels comfortable in their own skin. It is elegant and ostentatious! It speaks of money, power and of someone who has lots of confidence to carry it off. It is a mixing of the old antique bits with the new modern pieces. This combination takes courage and confidence to carry off. It represents, beautifully, those who seek more confidence to be themselves in life, rather than live under the shadow of someone else.

- Glamorous modern candle-holders hold large, yellow candles denoting holding power in your hands.
- The ram is associated with the chakra but this elaborate antique speaks of someone who is in control and likes to make a statement!
- The gold jewellery represents personal power.
- Sunstone and quartz crystals are associated with the chakra.
- Ylang ylang incense is the fragrance association.
- The yellow cloth is vibrant and energising and stimulates the sense of sight.
- The photo represents sight.
- The yellow candles, to the left, represent fire, which is the element of this chakra.

## Heart Chakra Altar

This simple alter sums up, beautifully, a person wanting to move on from the loss of a loved one. The loss can either be from bereavement or the end of a relationship. The jewellery box is open, representing the desire to open the heart chakra, which often closes down after it has been hurt.

- A wedding band and engagement ring is representative of wanting to find a loving, committed partner.
- Rose quartz is a healing heart stone bringing love into one's life, either of self or from a new partner.
- The red rose represents love and romance.
- The jewels are all heart crystals: green aventurine, moonstone and ruby. They could be gifts from loved ones or to ourselves, encouraging self-love.
- The perfume is rose to stimulate the senses.
- The peacock feather represents the sense of touch as it is very sensual.
- The pink cloth and green lining of the box represent love and healing at the same time.

## Throat Chakra Altar

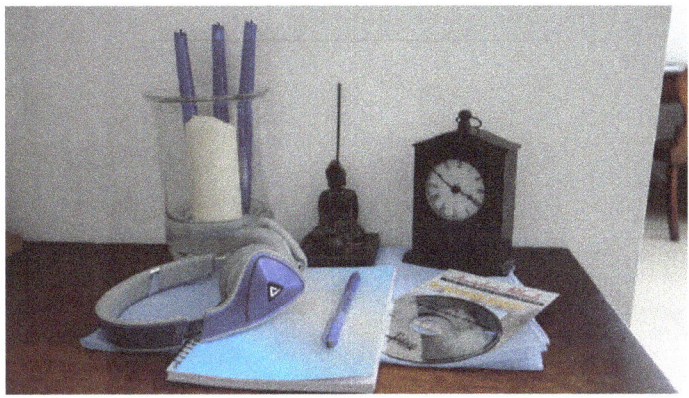

This is a very masculine altar. It represents someone who needs to open up their communication channels more and learn to listen! For relationships to work we need to have clear communication channels from both sides. When we lead busy lives we often rush around giving no time for quiet contemplation where we can listen to our guidance or guidance from those who are close.

- Headphones represent hearing and the ability to listen.
- A meditation CD is for reminding us that we need to relax each day so we can hear our own inner guidance.
- The clock represents time and reminds us to find time for ourselves.
- Chamomile incense represents relaxation.
- Blue and white candles bring in more light, both divine light and the blue ray of the throat.
- The notebook represents communication.
- The pale-blue cloth represents the throat chakra.

## Third Eye Chakra Altar

This is a simple spiritual-based altar. It is someone who is beginning to walk their spiritual path. It could be for either a male or female. It is uncluttered, with one pathway to follow!

- Spiritual books to assist, on one's spiritual path to ascension.
- Oracle cards representing the universe, third eye and triumph. These are representative of our wisdom and intuition.
- The universe and third eye oracle cards also represent the psychic archetype as well as the telepathic energy element.
- Celestite and sodalite crystals are third eye chakras.
- The sodalite angel represents the third eye communion with the angelic realms.
- The Buddha incense holder and rose geranium incense bring a sense of peace.
- The indigo cloth represents that dark blue of the third eye.

## Crown Chakra Altar

This altar is a feminine altar with a strong angelic connection. The person it represents wants to open up completely to the other higher dimensions, so they can walk their spiritual pathway with confidence.

- The water fountain represents the Aquarian influence of the water carrier.

- The Buddha in both the water fountain and incense holder represents the Guru archetype.

- Spirituality is represented by the angels, angel feathers and the fairy.
- Clear quartz, candle quartz, apopthylite and amethyst crystals are associated with the crown chakra and help to open it so that one can connect to the higher realms.
- Lavender incense induces a deep meditation as it is a very relaxing, calming smell to the senses.
- The purple stock flowers are a pretty reminder that we are all from the same source. We are all one.
- The white candle helps bring in more light as it represents the divine light.
- The pale purple cloth represents the crown chakra.

So, as you can see altars come in all shapes and sizes. They can be simple or elaborate. Just use your natural creativity to design what feels right for you...but most of all, have fun with it!

# Meditation

Meditation is a practice that involves stilling the mind to the point where it can stop all the external chatter that it processes every day. It can bring you to a deep state of relaxation. It is in this state of relaxation that we can connect to our inner voice, which is our voice of wisdom and intuition. Meditation has been found to have dramatic health effects on the body, especially on people who live in the fast lane and are continuously stressed. Our bodies can only take so much stress before they begin to show the signs of it. Sleeping patterns are disturbed, digestive problems abound, our skin ages more quickly, our muscles become tense and ache, we suffer from migraines and headaches, we become short tempered and we often have less time for friends and family. Once time is allowed for meditation and it becomes a daily ritual then you will find that you will move heaven and earth to make time for it! There are no set rules on how to meditate you just need to make sure of the following basics:

Turn your phone off or put it on silent!

Turn the TV off.

Make sure friends and family know what time you will be unavailable so that no one is likely to pop over.

Make it the same time every day so it becomes a ritual. Rituals are easier to stick by, but don't worry if you can't. You will just have to use more will power.

Wear comfortable clothing so that you can relax.

Make sure you are warm or you will fidget and find it hard to unwind.

Choose a comfortable chair or mat, if lying down.

Have a glass of water in case you need it. Sometimes when the throat chakra opens it can make us cough.

A bucketful of patience and love for yourself…so, if you don't succeed the first time, you won't give up.

Practice makes perfect and this is very true of meditation. Retraining our brain to be quiet is like trying to quiet a two-year-old after eating sweets! But it is worth it and the more you do it the easier it becomes.

- Make sure you are in a comfortable position and can relax. Making sure there will be no distractions out of the window for example!
- Ensure that anything you know needs to be done is sorted before you meditate or you will sit thinking about it instead of quieting the mind!
- Play some soft music in the background as this will help you to relax.
- Light a candle to mark the start of the meditation. Make sure that the candle is away from any fire hazards. A tea light in a holder works fine. This will trigger the body to know it is time to relax. Little rituals like this soon become habits, which will help you to relax more quickly each time.
- Start to breathe in through the nose and out through the nose. Place your hands on your tummy and feel the breath from here. This will ensure your breath is coming from the diaphragm and not from chest, ensuring a deep cleansing breath rather than a shallow one. It is very good for the body to breathe deeply as it clears out all the stale air and brings in more oxygen on the following breath.
- Breathe consciously in and out. Now on the 'in' breath, breathe in the feelings of peace. Feel or

imagine that peace filling the body. You can just imagine the word being breathed in; go with whatever feels natural to you. Don't worry if it feels difficult at first just persevere. Soon it will become easier.

- Now when you breathe out, breathe out any tension in the body. You can imagine the word, or just feel the tension leaving you.

- Continue to breathe in, peace, and out, tension. Do this for as long as feels natural for the body to begin to relax. You will soon start to feel the muscles relax in the body. The more you practice the faster you will feel the body responding. You can even clench each set of muscles and then relax them. Start with the feet. Tense them, then as you breathe out tension from the body relax them. Then tense the legs and repeat the action. Then clench the buttocks, stomach, hands, arms, shoulders, jaw, eyes and repeat to each set of muscles. By the time you get to the eyes you will be very relaxed!

- If any mental chatter enters your mind just let it gently float away. Don't stress about the mental chatter just imagine putting it in a bucket and letting it go.

- Continue to relax and quiet the mind.

- You can remain in this state for the length of time you have set yourself. Ten minutes is a good starting point. If you practice this for the first month, then you can increase the time 5 minutes at a time until you find it easy to spend an hour in quiet meditation.

This type of meditation can be practiced as often as you like. Every day would be ideal but if you can only manage 2-3 times a week then choose the same days each week.

Make it become a ritual and you are more likely to continue with it.

## Specific meditations for specific healings...

### Healing an illness meditation

Meditation can be used to focus on healing a specific illness in the body. It could be a time when you are really able to get in touch with the illness and 'ask' it why it has appeared. All illness has an emotional basis so finding the root cause can give you insights on how to clear the emotions, which, in turn, will help to heal the illness.

We can also send healing energy to any part of the body during meditation to help heal the problem. Emerald green light or divine, white light are both good colours to use, as they are the highest healing colours possible.

However, if you are drawn to send another colour to any area, go with your gut instinct. You may be drawn to send red, which would indicate that the area needing healing is very sluggish and needs warming up.

Blue would indicate that the area in need of healing is very inflamed and the blue ray is needed to cool the area down.

Pink on the other hand may indicate that you are sending the illness angry thoughts and it is in need of the pink ray of love. All illness in the body is a sign of an imbalance and, most importantly, it is a sign that you are not in balance, so if in doubt always send the area loving thoughts.

- Follow as before for meditation, but light a candle to match the colour of the healing light you are going to be using or use a white one.

- Continue to breathe in peace and out tension but concentrate on the illness you want to heal and where it is in the body. Breathe in healing green light (or the colour light you are drawn to use) and feel it travel down to the area of illness. Feel the colour surrounding the area. Feel it entering every cell and infusing the cells with healing light.

- Send the area loving thoughts and feel the connection with it. When this connection feels strong, ask the 'illness' why it has shown itself in your body. Listen and take note of any feelings, thoughts, ideas or pictures that come to mind. Keep these safe so they can be analysed after the meditation.

- Stay meditating for as long as you feel the need. Then thank the illness for showing its presence in your body and ask that it goes, as you have received its message.

- Gently bring yourself back to the present moment.

Remember the ideas, images or thoughts that came to you during the meditation and see if they spark any insight into why the illness has shown itself in the body. Write them down to see if they reoccur in another meditation session. Sometimes, if the same words are repeated, we can work out why the illness may be present.

Healing meditations will need to be repeated daily, if possible, or as many times a week as you have time for. The more you do the better, as it will bring the body into balance more quickly but, remember, illness sometimes takes a long time to manifest itself in the body and will take equally long to go! It will not be cured in five minutes. It takes dedication and a whole lot of self-love to bring about changes in the body.

Diet is also very important. If you want to bring about a healing in the body then you do need to cut out the bad foods such as processed foods, excessive coffee consumption, excessive alcohol consumption, sugary foods, white flour, fatty foods, etc. If you are drawn to seek the advice of a nutritionist to help you formulate a balanced healthy diet, then do so. What we put into our body can either heal or harm! Think of the scenario that you have a fabulous new car that has all the mod cons. Would you put poor quality petrol in it and expect it to perform well? No, you wouldn't dream of doing so, but we do it to our bodies! So before you put anything in your mouth, think .. *"is it going to heal or harm my body"*. This is a good way to make you more aware of what you are eating.

Fresh fruit and vegetables (both organic if possible), small amounts of lean organic meat, small amounts of wild-caught fish, nuts, seeds, and pulses are all foods that will help the body. Cakes, white flour, biscuits, sweets, fast food takeaways, processed foods (bacon, hams, sausages etc.), soda drinks and alcohol are foods that harm. Cutting out the harmful foods can be a bit of a challenge so cut them down slowly giving the body time to adjust to their removal from the diet. Sugary foods are one of the harder to remove because our body does become addicted to sugar. Cut these out by adding honey to tea or coffee. Try small amounts of dark chocolate instead of sweets. Small changes like these can help to lessen the withdrawal from sugar. Snacking on nuts instead of eating cakes or biscuits can help cut back sugar and white flour as well. There is a lot of information on the internet so take some time to research the good foods that will help your particular illness.

## Healing our emotions meditation

Follow the meditation instructions and light a candle with the colour you are drawn to. Blue is good when you want to draw in peace. Pink for love.

Breathe in the colour of the candle and concentrate on the emotion you want to heal.

Below is a short list of emotions to which you might relate. If the one you wish to clear is not on the list then add it, together with the positive one you want in its place

    Abandonment-Supported
    Anger-Peace
    Anxiety-Calm
    Betrayal-Being Loved
    Blame-Responsibility for self
    Confusion-Clarity
    Depression-Joy
    Disapproval-Optimism
    Disgust-Self love
    Failure-Success
    Fear- Confidence
    Forlorn-Upbeat
    Grief-Happiness
    Hatred-Love
    Heartache-Love
    Hopelessness-Hope
    Humiliation-Embraced
    Intimidation-Strength
    Insecurity-Security
    Jealousy-Happiness for others
    Lost-Knowing your way forward

Rejection-Acceptance
Sadness-Happiness
Sorrow-Joy
Stress-Relaxation
Vulnerability-Safety
Worthlessness-Worthiness

Now breathe in the positive emotion. An example would be to breathe in peace, this being the opposite emotion to anger. Feel peace filling your body from your feet to the top of your head. Now breathe out anger. Breathe it out from the whole body. Feel the anger leaving your body and imagine it being turned to loving energy. See the anger dissolving before your eyes! You may find it easier to see yourself breathing in the word peace and breathing out the word anger. Try different ways until you find a way that suits you.

Stay breathing in the positive emotion and breathing out the negative emotion for as long as you feel the need.

Gently bring yourself back to the present moment.

When we have any kind of relationship with another person we build a connection of energy with them. This connection comes in the form of a cord, which connects to the other person via one of the chakras. This cord will attach to a chakra according to what kind of relationship it is. If the other person gives us a house to live in, the cord could attach at the base chakra, our survival chakra. If the connection is purely for sexual reasons the cord will attach at the sacral chakra as this is our sex chakra. Connections at the solar plexus are usually from people who have knowledge to teach, or help empower us, such as teachers or gurus. The heart chakra is for love connections, either from lovers, family or close friends. The throat chakra is the communication chakra, where we learn to communicate things to the world. Platform speakers would send out cords to connect with their audiences. The third eye chakra is for spiritual connections to others. The crown chakra is our connection to the higher cosmos and would only connect to the higher levels rather than to another person.

We will all have many connections actively working on the front of the body via the energy chakra system. These are all healthy connections, transferring data between the people involved. When these connections of energy are helping us they remain connected and information in the form of energy will pass between them. The connection will be beneficial to both parties. This energy transference will help both souls to grow on the spiritual plane and learn lessons on this plane of existence. Once the flow ceases, the connection will remain but will no longer be active. Eventually, these connections will move to the back of both of the people's chakras and remain dormant until they disconnect naturally, by mutual consent. This will have little or no impact upon the health of either. This is how healthy connections are released.

However, there are cases where one person is unhappy about losing the connection. Perhaps it made them feel stronger as a person, or only complete when the other person was part of their life. They might have felt that the other person was the only person who could love, help or understand them. Alternatively, they could themselves have been an energy vampire, using the connection to draw energy off the other person. Energy vampires have lost or forgotten their ability to draw in energy from the universe and find it easier to steal someone else's. They are not usually aware of doing so, although some deliberately take energy to keep another person under their control. These are cases where the energy connection goes from being a healthy connection to being an unhealthy one. The connection will start at the front chakras but when one person isn't happy about the connection then their cord will move to their back while the one wanting to keep the connection will try to keep it open, at the front, and will be very unhappy when the connection is drawn away. They will know that the other person is trying to push them away and become less energised, feeling incomplete as a person, and at a loss.

This all usually occurs before any spoken words about parting company, so they will continue trying to reconnect, drawing energy from the other person so that everything remains as it was. Even after the other has stated their wish to leave and everything is over, at a point where the connection would normally slowly dissolve on both parties, they will continue to connect via the back chakra connection. The connection will then remain open because the disgruntled party will continue actively to connect here. This can be unhealthy if one of the connectors continues to draw energy from the other, who will experience tiredness as the most obvious result. Sleep makes little difference to how they feel – they keep waking feeling tired and low on energy. They may eventually think they have some illness causing it or may just accept this tiredness as a fact of growing older!

Although they may constantly think about the person from whom they have split, they won't understand why, as they are very happy the relationship is over but can't stop thoughts of them popping into their head for no obvious reason. They will make every effort to move on into a new life but still feel the past relationship pulling at them. This is because they literally are! They are disconnected from their end but not from the other; they are still very much connected even though it is to the back of the chakra. To the other person it feels the same…well, almost, in the sense that they will feel an energetic connection; they will not feel the loving connection as before.

When someone has finished a relationship that you wanted

to continue, you take what's on offer. This energetic connection does neither side any good. It is necessary to disconnect the energy cord from both parties but this can be difficult when one side is against it. If you feel that you are being held back by a prior relationship and find it hard to move on, it could be that you have an energy cord holding you back. This kind of connection can be severed during meditation if you hold to the intention of severing it. I have to add *'if'* because sometimes we feel flattered when someone can't let us go. It can make us feel empowered, knowing we hold this kind of control over someone. Unfortunately, it holds both parties back from moving on. The one who doesn't want the relationship to finish is being fed false hope energetically, that the relationship will be rekindled, while the one who finished the relationship is being held back because the uncut cords are leaking borrowed power. So it truly is a lose-lose situation.

So if you think you may have an energetic connection that you can't let go, then you need to face up to the situation in hand and truly move onto a happier, more positive sense of being.

## Severing the energetic bond meditation

Repeat instructions as for meditation but light a pink candle as it is the colour of unconditional love.

Once you are in a relaxed state.

Start to look down the back of the body and see if you can sense or see intuitively any form of connection. It may show as a cord of rope, barbed wire, steel cable, string, elastic or anything that is relevant to you. Or you may not see anything but sense or just know that there is a connection holding you back. Or if you are the person who can't let go look to cut your active cord going to the other person. You will be drawn or intuitively know which chakra it is going from.

Say "I ask that this bond of energy be severed permanently; it has no permission to stay attached. I send love and light to the owner but they may not stay attached to me in any way." You may feel the need to say it only once or a few times. Go with what you feel is right for you.

Imagine the cord being cut. You can visualise this as it being cut with a sword, scissors, knife etc. If you work with the angels, you can ask Archangel Michael to do the cutting for you. Either way just 'know' that it is done.

Stay in quiet relaxation while you centre yourself. Sometimes the cutting can bring feelings to the surface, sadness, grief, relief, anger. Whatever the emotions just breathe them out. Don't hold on to them as they are ready to be released. Let them go. If you feel you need to cry, do so. Whatever emotions are brought up let them go …breathe them out and say goodbye to them. They are no longer serving you and you are ready to release them.

When you feel centred and have released all that needs to be released, slowly bring your awareness back to the present.

Start to rub the hands on the legs to help ground you. Gently stamp the feet on the floor.

Now state out loud, *I am a divine spark of light and, as such, I am perfect as I am.* This helps to reinforce the fact that you can cope without the energetic connection that you have just released.

This meditation can be repeated to clear as many past connections as you feel you need to release. Sometimes a connection can reattach if you haven't totally accepted the release and you inadvertently let the other person attach again. If so just keep releasing until you feel intuitively that the connection is severed permanently. This can be any number of times depending on you! If you are the dependent person that is trying to let go then keep severing the connection until you feel you no longer need the connection to the other person. This will usually show as you not thinking about them on a daily basis. The other person won't haunt your thoughts and you will feel a freedom that you hadn't felt before. This will be a sign to you that you have truly let the other person go and you can now move on in your life and find the happiness you deserve.

## Healing our inner child meditation

We all have an inner child. It is the childlike part of us that develops before we hit puberty. If we go through a challenging childhood, then our inner child can become hurt and angry. It can retreat inside us and go into hiding. It's a bit like taking all our childhood problems and putting them into a box and storing it in our hearts. The box can stay there but if an event crosses our path that reminds us of our childhood the box can pop open without warning and start a whirlwind of emotions pouring out. As children we deal with things simply as we don't have the knowledge of an adult. Events during childhood, which seem huge and scary, would be less distressing and, in some cases, quite funny, to an adult. These emotions need to be viewed through adult eyes and released. This can be a scary process as we are dealing with our childlike self and the emotions we felt then but, if we give our inner child lots of love and listen to it, we can clear past emotions. If you find the process very painful then you may wish to use a therapist to guide you through a clearing procedure or have a good friend with you rather than face it alone. It is your body and you need to have trust in what you think is right.

Follow meditation, as before, then ask your inner child to show itself. You may see a child appear in your mind's eye.

Or you may have to imagine a small child sitting in front of you. It doesn't matter as the fact you are acknowledging that your inner child is there will be enough for you to do this meditation.

Smile at the child and ask them what it is that needs to be released, healed or acknowledged. Words may pop into your head or you may feel emotions such as sadness. Gently accept these feelings. Ask your inner child to show you everything that needs to be cleared. If you feel emotions welling up inside you, let them out. There might be tears, perhaps of anger. Have a box of tissues ready for the tears and, maybe, a pillow or cushion to thump if any angry feelings arise and you want relief. You may want to write down your feelings and, at the end of the meditation, rip them up to release the feelings. Find a way that feels right for you but accept the existence of the feelings and release them.

If they are too overwhelming, then gently thank your inner child for helping you and come out of the meditation. You can try another day when you will feel better able to cope with the emotions.

If you can go on, then do so.

We can have conversations with our inner child.

We can let our inner child know that it was ok to have such feelings but now, as an adult, you can gently let them go.

Talk to your inner child as you would if a child came to you with questions or problems.

The fact that the inner child is you doesn't matter. The fact that you are listening and taking notice will help to clear past problems.

Several mediations may be needed to release all the emotions. This doesn't matter just go with the flow of what you feel is right. You may want to deal with one issue at a time or may try to clear all at once. Your body will guide you, learn to listen to it and trust it.

When you feel you have released all that needs to be released slowly bring your awareness back to the present.

Start to rub the hands on the legs to help ground you. Gently stamp the feet on the floor.

After the meditation you may feel drawn to write your feelings down in a journal. You may find that more things surface a few days after the clearing. Gently let these emotions flow out. You may also want to reinforce the release of the emotions by writing them on paper that you can then rip up or burn. By taking a shower after the meditation you can imagine the water cleansing all the emotions away. You can also call in the angels to help you clear any residue emotions. Just imagine them surrounding you and gently ask them to cleanse your inner child.

Remember, anything worth having in life usually takes time and effort. So it is with meditation. Practice, practice, PRACTICE! Then one magical day it will just click and your mental chatter will stop the moment you sit and start. Trust me...I have been there!

# Visualisation

This powerful tool can be used to draw into our life anything that we want. Yes, you heard me right...anything! In fact, it is such a powerful tool that all great business men and women use it on a daily basis to help them achieve their goals. It is a simple process *but*, and yes there is a but! You have to have total belief that it will work; that is the hard part!! It took me time, working at it, but in the end I got there.

Now, you remember in earlier chapters about how our thoughts are energy and, as such, we draw into our life what we experience: ill health, unhappiness etc.? Well, this is using a similar process but with a slight twist. In this exercise we 'see' what we want to have in our life. So, for example, if you would like to have a happy, lasting, fulfilling relationship, then you sit and spend time visualising the person you would like in your life.

You visualise all the traits you would like him/her to have and you see yourself happy. Or if you would like a nicer house to live in then visualise it, or if you want vibrant health see yourself fit and healthy. The more details you 'see', the better as you are actively building a picture of your dreams and co-creating them at the same time!

If you take time, say ten minutes daily, to visualise, then it will give you a good start. As you begin to feel more comfortable, thinking of what you want, you can increase the time, up to thirty minutes daily.

Now the secret to success is to begin to feel as if you have already got what you want. So if you want a new relationship make sure that you have space to have someone in your life. Get into a routine of cleaning the house as if you had them coming over to stay. Keep that special bottle of wine for when they do come. Plan what meal you would like to prepare them. Or if you want vibrant health then start to treat yourself to life enhancing organic foods. Plan where you would like to visit when you are well enough and you can even set a date in your calendar to visit it in a few weeks or months depending on the severity of your health problem. Plan the trip and what you want to do when the date arrives. Or if you want a new house, start deciding which area you would like to live in, how many bedrooms, bathrooms and the colours you would like to paint it when you move in.

The more details the better. Now start to sense those feelings as if you already have what you wish for. How would it change your life? How would you feel? How would your body feel? At first you will have to make yourself feel these things or guess at how you will feel but, after a while, you will truly notice a difference in your body. You may feel excitement, peace, happiness, joy or any number of other things. You can keep a notebook to jot down ideas, when visualising your dreams into reality, as new ideas pop into your head.

Now I hear you thinking *'well that's all well and dandy but, if it worked, wouldn't everyone be doing it?'* Well they would if they held total belief that what they wished for came true, but, when they don't get instant results people lose faith and this is where they fail. As soon as you lose the faith then the energy stops flowing. Your own doubt halts the process. It can be likened to a light bulb. When the current is flowing (your active ideas) then the bulb shines brightly but, as soon as you stop visualising it's the same as someone turning the switch off and stopping the flow of electricity. The bulb goes dim and ceases to shine; your dreams are put on hold.

Visualisation comes under the law of attraction, which is a

universal law or, to put it another way, it is a law of nature. We are all subject to this law but, as I have already mentioned, not everyone uses it properly. It is a law stating that whatever we think about we will attract. So negative thoughts such as lack of money, not enough food, useless partners, horrible houses will attract similar unhappy energies. Any money that comes to you will quickly have to be used on something such as an unexpected bill. The universe won't hear 'I don't like this house' it will only hear 'like this house' so you will be thwarted at every turn, because your thoughts will be creating your reality and your thoughts are much more powerful than you think they are.

So check, and be sure that you think 'I have an abundance of money, I have the perfect house for me'. This way you will be visualising what you want and feeling the effects of having it and, before you know it, you will have your dream. Like attracts like …so let your thoughts dwell only on good things and only good things will come. Remember this simple four step process:

- Visualise – See what it is that you want. Get a clear picture in your head. See it in the smallest details. Feel as if you already have it. Live it and breathe it when you visualise it. The more real you make it, the better.

- Believe – Have total trust that it is coming to you. Start planning, declutter the house in readiness for that move, plan that holiday, mentally spend that money! Tell everyone what you have ordered from the universe! Tell them that it's coming and that they will see the results when they arrive. Buy that bottle of bubbly to celebrate when your dream arrives! The more belief you have, the better, as belief is a positive energy.

- Get ready to receive – Feel good about the prospect of your dream coming true. Hold those feelings each and every day as many times as you can remember to take five minutes out to do so. Feel those happy thoughts flowing through you knowing that it will happen and it will arrive with perfect timing. The happier those thoughts are, the better you will feel each day, and happy thoughts attract positive energy to you, which will attract your dream even quicker.

- Don't doubt – It will take as long as it needs to happen because the universe knows the optimum time better than we do. So if it doesn't arrive when you think it should, just remind yourself that it will be even better when it comes. So, if your dream house goes, don't stress, because a better one is coming along. If your health doesn't improve as quickly as you hoped, it's because you need to rest a little longer; when your health returns you can do all those activities you have been putting off. If the money doesn't arrive for that holiday, then you are not meant to be going on it, as it wouldn't have been as good as you thought it would be and the money is coming for something better!

You have to remember that once you activate the energy of creation with your thoughts, some things take longer than others, if many other factors are involved. The universe will be actively working behind the scenes, setting up everything for your dream to come true. The universe cannot abide a vacuum and when you create a thought of what you want it has to fill that thought. The only time it doesn't is if you decide your dream is not coming!

The best way to put this simple process into practice is to start with something small. Say you need a parking space one day for something important. Start to visualise getting the perfect parking space a couple of weeks beforehand. See it and feel the relief you feel when you know you have just parked your car in it. Or try visualising something small coming into your life, maybe a bunch of flowers. Decide what type you would like and their colour then see the flowers. Smell them. See them in your house looking pretty. Once you start to see the little things happen, you get the confidence and belief to try for the bigger things. If at first it doesn't happen just know that somewhere you didn't really believe it would, so be sure to clear those thoughts out of your head and start again. One day it will happen and it will give you the belief to go for bigger things. Persevere. Expecting the best each day builds a positive attitude... Can you think of a better way to live?!!

## Vision boards

These are a creative way to visualise your dreams. They work on the same principle as visualisation but the only difference is that you create your vision on a piece of paper or card. So if you want to attract money into your life you would cut out pictures of money and things that you want the money for and stick them creatively on a piece of card or paper. The size doesn't matter it's the creative energy that you are creating that counts, by making the vision board. You can create an elaborate board or just place a few relevant pictures. You don't have to be artistic as it's only your representation of what you want.

When you have created your board you can place it in a prominent place so that every time you pass it you think about what you want. You can also spend time sitting with it, visualising the things you want, as in the visualisation process above. You can create different boards for different things or put it all on one board. Let your imagination run wild and have fun while you do it. Once you have attracted part of what you want in life you can replace the pictures with something else or create a new board.

Here are some ideas for pictures you can use for your vision board:

- Money – pictures of notes, coins, treasure chest of money.

- Holiday – picture of beaches with palm trees, pyramids, aeroplanes, 5-star hotels, pictures of capital cities, or specific picture of destination.

- Health issues – athletes, gym, yoga class, football, people running, people rowing, happy smiling fit person, old picture of you when you were healthy.

- Healthier lifestyle – fresh fruit and vegetables, pictures of vegetable gardens, raw nuts, raw seeds, pulses, glasses of water, plates of salads, fruit trees laden with healthy fruit.

- Spiritual growth – third eye chakra, crown chakra, or pictures of all the chakras, crystals, Buddha or other deity, Angels, peaceful scenes in nature, yoga poses in nature, symbols that resonate with you, archetypal symbols or animals.

- New career or job – name of company you would like to work for, title of position you want, pictures of big companies, pictures of newspapers for journalists, magazines etc. that you want to write for, pictures of the country and their currency if you want to work abroad.

- Car – picture of car you want, colour swab of colour of car you want, or logo of type of car you want.

- New image – hairstyles you like, make up, clothes you like, jewellery, shoes, celebrities you like, bags.

- Weight loss/gain – pictures of fit, healthy-looking people you wish you were like, old pictures of you, fit athletes, fresh fruit and vegetables, healthy meals, your goal weight.

- New house – pictures of styles you like, mansions (why not!), furniture, colour swabs for the walls, bathroom fittings, kitchen units, interior designs.

- Wedding – pictures of churches, wedding rings, weddings dresses, horse and carriage, wedding car, wedding flowers, pictures of celebrities' weddings.

- Relationship – pictures of people who have similar traits to the person you would like in your life, handsome men, beautiful women, couples holding hands, couples kissing, words of the traits you would like in a person, hairstyle, dress style, if you are looking for a sporty person pictures of people doing sporty things etc.

- Miscellaneous – Ipad, Ipod, computer, phone, TV, CD player, DVD player, gold/silver jewellery, restaurants, cinemas, theme parks, perfume, aftershave, shopping bags from favourite stores.

These are just a few ideas to get you started. Anything that has a meaning to you can be used to create your own vision board. Magazines, newspapers, photos or the internet can be used to obtain the pictures that you want. You can use plain white card or paper or choose your favourite colour. I like to arrange the pictures first before I stick them so I get an idea of what they look like together, I play around with the images until I find a design that I like then attack with the glue stick! Place the finished board in a place where you will see it frequently. Every time you pass you feel a few moments of pleasure at having the things you have asked for. You can even sit looking at in meditation or visualisation.

# Gratitude

Just a quick bit about gratitude because this is as important as visualisation. "Thank you" are only two little words but they have a huge impact on us. When we help someone or give someone a gift we like to have a thank you. It shows that the receiver is grateful for the gift and makes us feel happy and good that we have made the effort. When we give someone a gift and no response is forthcoming we feel upset that after making an effort to do a good deed it is not appreciated. It also makes us reluctant to do it again!

This is the same with universal law. We are given many gifts every day but we usually don't think about them consciously. Examples would be things such as a friend popping by to say 'hi'. It brings us a warm, happy feeling when someone has thought about us. Someone in the street says 'have a good day' and, again, we feel happy inside. Both of these are gifts that brighten our day but we wouldn't really think of them as such. Start to become more aware of the gifts that you are given every day, because the more grateful we are for what we receive in life, the more we open ourselves to receive again. This is because, from a spiritual perspective, the universe likes gratitude and, from an earthly perspective, when we start to be thankful for things in our life we feel happy and are actively creating a positive energy cloud around us. This positive energy cloud makes us feel good and attracts good energy to us, which can be in the form of nice people or nice things happening to us. The more that nice things happen, the more belief we have that the universe is abundant.

Have you ever walked down the street and someone for no

reason has smiled at you? It makes you feel happy for the rest of the day. It leaves that tiny seed of happy energy that lingers and sets you up for having a good day. You in turn will smile at someone else and so the ripple effect goes out and touches other people. This is a bit like gratitude. The more things we are grateful for, the more things we find we have to be grateful for, and sometimes we even start to help people in order to feel even happier that others are feeling as good as we are!

So start taking a few minutes at night to list five things for which you are grateful. They can be anything that is important to you. A friend popping by to say 'hi', a sunny day, a friendly smile, a great cup of coffee, money in your purse, a roof over your head, a hot meal, a bed ...an umbrella when it's raining! There is always something to be grateful for.

I have a gratitude crystal next to my bed. I hold it each night and say thank you for all the good things that happen to me each day. Even when I've had a day from hell I always make myself be thankful for something. It might be having my electric blanket warming my bed in the winter months, which is one thing I'm always grateful for – it is one of the best inventions ever!! Or it might be gratitude for having arms and legs, to do everyday things. It may be having the sight to see this wonderful world around me.

Remember, there is always something to be grateful for. You may find yourself listing more than five, which is great, as there is no limit on the number of things you can be grateful for.

The most important 'thank you' is made when your dream comes true! Do not forget that one, or the universe might not bring it so quickly next time!

\*\*\*

# Well my friends

I have given you the tools which I used to pull me out of my darkest times and put me onto the road to a new, happier me. Some of my tools might not resonate with you. If they don't, then don't use them. Always work with the ones that do resonate. Each of us has a different approach to bringing back our inner balance and power, so use the tools that feel good for you because this is your healing. It is the time for you to think about and concentrate on yourself. The journey will take as long as is needed for you.

Everyone travels their journey in their own time. There is no right or wrong about how long it takes! My journey took me two years and lots of soul-searching, time, patience and self-love.

I had support from family and friends and for that I am eternally grateful but even if I hadn't, I know I would have got there eventually, it may have taken me longer though!

My angels were also there to help me with a hug and to wrap me in loving energy when I needed it. So this journey can be made with just your angels, if you don't have any friends or family around you. Friends and family made my journey easier when I needed a shoulder to cry on or a kick up the arse!! I think my mum gave me a few of those!! But I got there and now live a life I could not have dreamed possible.

I have a loving family and a loving partner. I had my ups and downs along the path as will you. Some days I still do, but I've reached the place I wanted to be and I am now a far stronger person, who knows she can and will accomplish anything she sets her mind to! Just remember, if you have a setback, laugh it off and know that tomorrow is another day. I lost count of how many setbacks I had but, each time, I picked myself up and carried on, as you will do. Just remember not to get angry with yourself. Cry, rant and rave at the mirror, beat up that pillow, but don't blame yourself. Setbacks are all part of the learning journey. You will get to the end …trust me. You will!

So use this book with my blessings, to help you along your own personal road. Go with the flow of life and embrace each and every hurdle knowing that you will make it and come out a stronger, happier more harmonious person.

Love, Light and Blessings my Friends.

Tamsin xx

# INDEX

Abundantia, 163

Additional chakras, 53

Agate, 81

Altar examples, 202

Amazonite, 84

Amber, 85

Amethyst, 86

Angels, 148

Apache Tear, 126

Apatite, 87

Aquamarine, 89

Aragonite, 90

Archangel Ariel, 150

Archangel Azrael, 150

Archangel Chamuel, 151

Archangel Gabriel, 151

Archangel Haniel, 152

Archangel Jeremiel, 152

Archangel Jophiel, 153

Archangel Metatron, 153

Archangel Michael, 153

Archangel Raguel, 154

Archangel Raphael, 155

Archangel Raziel, 155

Archangel Sandalphon, 156

Archangel Uriel, 156

Archangel Zadkiel, 157

Ascended masters., 162

Atala, 49

Athena, 163

Aventurine, 91

Azurite, 93

Babaji, 163

Base chakra, 40

BASE/ROOT CHAKRA, 196

Base/Root Chakra Altar, 202

Black, 174

Black calcite, 97

Black Obsidian, 126

Black Tourmaline, 94

Bloodstone, 95

Blue Aventurine, 92

Blue calcite, 97

Blue fluorite, 109

Blue Lace Agate, 82

Blue Quartz, 132

Blue Tiger's Eye, 141

Blue topaz, 143

BLUE, INDIGO and VIOLET FOODS, 192

Brigit, 163

Brown, 174

Brown Jasper and Picture Jasper, 114

Buddha, 163

Calcite, 96

Caring for your crystals, 78

Carnelian, 99

Celestite, 100

Chalcedony, 101

Characteristics of the colours, 168

Charoite, 103

Chart showing the minor chakras and their associations in the body, 52

Choosing Crystals, 75

Chrysoprase, 104

Citrine, 105

Clear calcite, 97

Clear topaz, 143

Colour breathing, 179

Colour breathing for mental well-being, 180

Colour breathing technique, 179

Colour table for mental and emotional dis-ease, 181

Colour table for physical dis-ease, 178

Colour wheel, 167

Coloured silks, 179

Complementary colours, 166

Crown, 47

CROWN CHAKRA, 200

Crystals, 71

Crystals and the Zodiac, 75

Dalmatian Jasper, 114

Diamond, 106

Earth chakra, 53

Eating colour, 188

El Morya, 163

Emerald, 107

Flamingo Jasper, 114

Fluorite, 108

Garnet (red), 110

Gold calcite, 97

Golden topaz, 144

Gonads, 58

Gratitude., 236

Green, 171

Green Aventurine, 92

Green calcite, 97

Green fluorite, 109

GREEN FOODS, 191

Green Jasper, 115

Healing an illness meditation, 216

Healing our emotions meditation., 219

Healing our inner child meditation, 225

Heart, 44

HEART CHAKRA, 198

Heart Chakra Altar, 208

Hematite, 111

Herkimer diamonds, 106

Higher crown chakra, 53
How to use crystals, 73
Howlite, 112
Indigo, 172
Isolt, 163
Jasper, 113
Jesus, 163
Kuan Yin, 163
Kyanite, 116
Labradorite, 117
Lapis Lazuli, 118
Lepidolite, 120
List of the archangels, their associated crystals and what areas they cover., 158
Magenta, 174
Mahatala and Patala, 51
Mahogany Obsidian, 127
Malachite, 122
Meditating with colour, 182
Meditating with coloured silks, 183
Meditation, 213
Merlin, 163
Mookaite Jasper, 115
Moonstone, 124
Moses, 163
Moss agate, 83
Mother Mary, 163
Obsidian, 125
Onyx, 128
Orange, 169
Orange calcite, 97
ORANGE FOODS, 190
Pale Blue, 172
Pancreas, 59
Past life chakra, 54
Petrified Wood, 129
Pineal gland, 62
Pink calcite (Mangano calcite), 98
Pink topaz, 144
Pituitary, 61
Prehnite, 130
Primary colours, 166
Purple fluorite, 109
Quartz, 131
Rasatala, 50
Red, 169
Red calcite, 98
RED FOODS, 190
Red Jasper and Brecciated Jasper, 115
Rhodochrosite, 134
Rhodonite, 135
Rose Quartz, 132
Ruby, 136
Rutilated Quartz, 133
Sacral chakra, 41
SACRAL CHAKRA, 196
Sacral Chakra Altar, 204
Saint Francis, 163

Saint John of God, 163
Saint Padre Pio, 164
Sanat Kumara, 164
Secondary colours, 166
Serapis Bay, 164
Severing the energetic bond meditation, 223
Smoky Quartz, 133
Snowflake Obsidian, 127
Sodalite, 137
Solar Plexus, 43
SOLAR PLEXUS CHAKRA, 197
Spirit guides, 160
Spleen chakra, 53
Sugilite, 138
Sunstone, 139
Sutala, 49
Talatala, 50
Tertiary colours, 166
The Adrenal Glands, 56
The fifth or Etheric Template Body, 35
The first layer or Etheric Body, 30
The fourth layer or Astral Level, 34
The Lower Chakras, 49
The Major Chakras and their associations in the body, 48
The second layer or the Emotional Body, 31
The seventh or Causal Body, 37
The sixth or the Celestial Body, 36

The third layer or the Mental Body, 33
Third Eye, 46
Third Eye Chakra Altar, 210
THIRD EYE/BROW CHAKRA, 199
Throat Chakra, 45
THROAT CHAKRA, 198
Throat Chakra Altar, 209
Thymus, 59
Thyroid/Parathyroid, 60
Tiger's Eye, 140
Tigers Iron, 142
Topaz, 143
Turquoise, 173
Unakite, 145
Using coloured water, 176
Violet, 173
Vision boards., 232
Visualisation, 228
Visualisation with colour, 185
Visualisation with colour 2, 187
Vitala, 49
Vywamus, 164
Wearing colour, 175
White, 175
Yellow, 170
Yellow calcite, 98
YELLOW FOODS, 190

www.ingramcontent.com/pod-product-compliance
Lightning Source LLC
Chambersburg PA
CBHW040327300426

44113CB00020B/2680